THE RED
ABALONE SHELL

THE RED ABALONE SHELL

FRANCES SCHOONMAKER

Frances Schoonmaker

The Last Crystal Trilogy, book 2

Illustrated by the author

Auctus Publishers
Havertown, Pennsylvania, United States

AucTus Publishers
606 Merion Ave, First Floor
Havertown, PA 19083, USA

Softcover ISBN 978-0-9979607-7-8
Hardcover ISBN 978-0-9979607-8-5
Electronic ISBN 978-0-9979607-9-2

for Liesl
daughter, wise counselor,
and friend

Acknowledgments

Thanks to Amelia Bolin, junior editor and co-conspirator, who has seen the book through its many drafts. (It wouldn't have been nearly as much fun without you). Nathaniel Storck, thanks for your help (especially when there are so many other interesting things to do on a day off.) Warren Schoonmaker, thanks for help with the cover and wise counsel. (I still say you are a better brother than Junior Swathmore—or Hiram Swathe, for that matter.) Thanks again to Isaiah Laich and Sarah VanTiem, for reading the first draft. (Your have offered unfailingly good advice and encouragement along the way.) Thanks to Jon Dunlap and Katie Schmidt. (If there were such a thing as a Super-Hero Teachers Award, you'd both hold it.)

Additionally, Marianne Babal, Senior Corporate Historian, Wells Fargo Corporate Heritage provided information about bank notes in the late 1800s. The quotation from Woodrow Wilson's Flag Day speech in Chapter 19 is from *The President's Flag Day Address With Evidence Of Germany's Plans,* The Committee on Public Information, September 15, 1917. See http://libcdm1.uncg.edu/cdm/ref/collection/WWIPamp/id/23446.

Finally, thanks to all of you who have read *The Black Alabaster Box* and gently nagged me for Book 2.

Book cover photograph and design by Liesl Bolin.

CONTENTS

PREFACE

The Black Alabaster Box tells how Grace Willis reluctantly left for California with her family in 1856, following the Santa Fe Trail from Kansas City. When Small Pox strikes the wagon train, her mother falls victim. The Willis wagon is forced to stay behind. Just when she thinks her mother is getting well, Grace is kidnapped by the ruthless Hiram Swathmore and his whining wife, taken into Oklahoma Territory, and forced to work like a slave. They tell her that both her parents died of the Pox, but Grace is suspicious. The Swathmore twins, Ruby and Junior, delight in her misery, taunting her unmercifully. Her only friend is a dog, Old Shep. Grace decides to run away and search for her parents, but circumstances force her to leave before she is ready. With Mr. Sawthmore tracking her down, Old Shep urges Grace on until she is rescued by the mysterious Mr. Nichols. He seems to know her and Old Shep. Another adventure begins, even more dangerous than the one she encountered on the Trail. Grace learns that there is such a thing as magic and there are some things that only a child can do.

The Red Abalone Shell begins with Grace's son, James. In the interest of the story, I have altered the time line, moving it forward by about twenty years. This alteration of time is not magic at work. I have tried to keep the history as true as possible, given what we know to date about events of the late 19th and early 20th centuries. But I needed to situate the story at the beginning of World War I.

Junior and Ruby reappear in this book. They have an encounter with the Dalton Brothers near The Alabaster Caverns. Even more famous than Junior and Ruby, the Daltons terrorized the American Old West between 1890-1892 when a shoot-out at Coffeyville, Kansas put an end to the gang. The Caverns were used as a hideout by several outlaw gangs before they were "discovered" and became a tourist attraction. Tradition has it that one of the gangs was the Dalton Brothers. It makes a good story whether or not the Daltons ever hid out there. You can find out more about the Daltons Gang at the Oklahoma Historical Society website. Look for Nancy B. Samuelson, "Dalton Gang,"

http://www.okhistory.org/publications/enc/entry.php?entryname=DALTON%20GANG

Note that when I refer to James's birth mother, Grace Willis, I use Mamma. Hanalore Matthias, his adoptive mother, is German-American. I use Mama when referring to her.

When I set out to write *The Red Abalone Shell*, I had an idea, my grandmother's ink well made from an abalone shell, and family stories to go on. My Grandpa Shannon testified to the good character of a German-American neighbor who was accused of being disloyal to the United

States during World War I. My mother remembered collecting peach pits with other school children—they were used in making gas masks worn during the war. As I searched for the broader story of which my family stories are a part, I learned that many German-Americans were persecuted during World War I. Organizations such as the National Security League and American Protective League fanned the fires of patriotism and squelched dissent.

My research for the *Trilogy* has included all kinds of interesting experiences in addition to library research. These range from visiting the National Frontier Trails Museum in Independence, Missouri, to taking the AMTRAK Southwest Chief train (successor to the Santa Fe Chief) from Kansas City to Los Angeles, to visiting the site of the Wishtoyo Chumash Village at Nicholas Canyon County Beach in Malibu, California.

There is more information about my research as well as resources on my website and blog:

www.fschoonmaker.com

www.fourleavesandtales.blog

I talk about the back-story of each of the books in *The Last Crystal Trilogy.*

Chapter 1

JAMES FOUND

James woke up to find himself sitting on the steps of a church, his arm around a big black and white dog. Nothing around him looked familiar. He had no idea where he was or how he got there. He wasn't sure how old he was and he couldn't remember his birthday. In fact, he didn't even know who he was, except that his name was James and the dog's name was Old Shep.

In one hand, he held an old map all rolled up and tied around with a string. A tag hanging from the string, read, "To my dear James, Love no end, Mamma," but he couldn't think who his mother was or what she looked like. In the other hand was a large, red shell. The inside was iridescent silver-white with green and deep blue. It was beautiful, but he had no idea why he was holding it.

Chapter 1

He was trying to think what to do when a horse and buggy pulled up to the church. A man and woman got out. They were all dressed up in their Sunday best. They were even more surprised to see him than he was to see them.

"Well, James," said the woman after they got over their initial surprise. "I'll bet there is one thing you can remember. That's breakfast. Mr. Matthias and I are in charge of opening the church this morning. I think he can take care of that. I'm taking you home and feeding you some breakfast."

Mr. Matthias agreed. "You and Old Shep can stay with us until we find your family," he said. "Don't you worry, Son, we'll do everything we can to find your people. We'll start by asking around at church this morning. Hannalore, I'll get a ride back home. James probably needs a good rest more than he needs a sermon."

Mr. Matthias asked around. Nobody seemed to know how James got there or who he was. It was if he had been deposited on the steps of the church by magic.

They took him to the doctor in Cedar Hills, the market town about twelve miles away. After giving James a thorough examination, the doctor said, "I see no evidence of a blow to your head. Maybe you experienced something traumatic. That can cause amnesia, too. There is every reason to believe that this is temporary. I think you will find that your memory begins to return.

I'm not sure how to judge your age. Everybody sets their own pace in growing. My guess is that you must be about twelve or thirteen. Does that sound right to you?"

James wasn't sure either. He didn't know what to think.

Turning to Mr. and Mrs. Matthias, the doctor said, "I'd like to see the boy again in about a month. Meanwhile, if you start to have headaches or feel too anxious, James, you must let me know." Advertisements were put in the local and state papers. The Sherriff and State Police were informed. A year passed.

James began to remember things, but his memories were fleeting and didn't seem to fit together. His family was never found. But he got on so well with Hannalore and Karl Matthias, that they adopted him as their own son. Since he couldn't remember his birthday, Mama made a cake for him to celebrate the day he was found. She said he was the best thing that had ever happened to them. Papa agreed.

One morning James stood looking at the shell. He kept it on his dresser. At school he learned that it was an abalone shell. *Abalone are found along the coast of California*, he thought. Then it came to him, *Somebody gave it to me and told me I must never forget. But who? What was I supposed to remember? Have I been to California?* He ran into a blank space in his mind.

Chapter 1

So far he remembered very little from the time before he was James Matthias. He was James somebody else then and he had a little sister. But something happened to the sister. He couldn't remember. Now he had a baby sister named Margaret Gracc who was nearly one-year-old.

"My mother's name was Grace," he said when they talked about naming the baby.

"Then Grace must be her middle name," said Mama. "Grace is a beautiful name."

James remembered in flashes like that. Each memory flash was like a piece in a gigantic puzzle. But he didn't have very many pieces. Every time he remembered, Mama and Papa encouraged him. "There is love enough to go around," Mama would say. She told him he could love his birth parents and all the memories of the time before and still have enough love to share with them. So he tried to remember. But he couldn't.

The map he had with him on the church steps now hung above his bed. The tag that said, "To James," was tucked away among his most precious treasures. Sometimes he took it out and studied it, wondering what his mother looked like and who his father was.

The map wasn't like any map he had ever studied in school. It had mountains and rivers and an ocean. But it didn't look like a real place you could go to or where you could live, at least not today. There were no roads marked on it, for one thing. Around the whole map was a border of delicately drawn plants and animals. Some looked familiar, like the buffalo and bear. Others reminded him of American Indian drawings. There was even a red abalone shell. All the drawings were painted with watercolor. He wondered if his mother was an artist. Maybe it was a place she imagined.

James put down the abalone shell, hurrying downstairs to help Papa with morning chores. Old Shep was waiting at the back door. There was always plenty to do on the farm. Old Shep was a willing helper. Maybe they'd lived on a farm before. Papa thought so because Old Shep seemed to know exactly what was expected. "He's the smartest dog I've ever known. There's something about him," Papa said. "I'm not sure how to describe it. Maybe 'wise' is the word. Old Shep is wise."

James wondered if Old Shep remembered. "Maybe you could tell me everything I want to know, if I could just talk doggie talk or if you could talk people talk," he said, heading for the barn. Old Shep looked at him as if he understood perfectly. Sometimes James thought that maybe Old Shep could talk, but chose not to. It wasn't something James was prepared to talk about, not even with his family. It was too fantastical. Even if he couldn't talk, Old Shep understood. There was something magical about him, too, something James couldn't quite put his finger on. He was wise, like Papa said, but there was more to it.

The sun was already on its way up. It promised to be a glorious day. Before breakfast the cows were milked and turned out to pasture, the chickens were fed, and pails of milk were poured into the large bowl of the separator that stood in a little room just off the back porch. After breakfast, Papa would turn the handle of the separator and the whole milk would separate into skimmed milk and cream. Mama used the cream in cooking and to make butter. There was plenty of skimmed milk for cooking, to make cheese, and to drink.

Mama had a grave look on her face when they came in to wash up. "I was just looking at yesterday's newspaper. The news gets worse every day. It seems like Germany is trying to gobble up all of Europe."

"I hope President Wilson stays firm about keeping us out of war," said Papa, filling the white enamel wash pan from the kitchen pump. "War just leads to more war."

Karl and Hannalore Matthias were pacifists. They believed that war under any circumstance was wrong and contrary to the Ten Commandments. Long ago, before Karl and Hannalore were born, their parents were among German pacifists who immigrated to the United States to escape religious persecution and being forced to serve in the army. Karl and Hannalore were both second generation German-Americans. They were born in the United States.

"Freedom of religion is protected by the United States Constitution," Papa liked to say. "That is a priceless treasure." Like most German immigrant families, they were fiercely proud to be American.

"You know we're in a minority, Karl," said Mamma, putting the coffee pot on the table. "Most of our friends think the US should help stop the Kaiser now that England has declared war." Wilhelm II was Kaiser, or Emperor of the German Empire. For years tension had been building up between European countries until war broke out in August of 1914.

Papa sighed as he dried his hands and face. "I think the world has more to fear from his generals than from the Kaiser himself, despite all his war talk. He's relied too much on his military to make policy. It will bring him down in the end."

"Either way, it's bad for us," said Mama. "An article in the paper said that there are supposed to be German spies living all over the country, ready to help take over the United States."

"Sensationalism," Papa sat down and poured himself a cup of coffee. "Long on emotion, short on facts. Mind you, that isn't to say there aren't German sympathizers—some of them may be prepared to do mischief—but to accuse everyone because of the few goes against everything this nation is supposed to stand for."

With so much talk of war, many families from Germany changed their names to make them sound more "American." Papa said that was ridiculous. He liked to say, "America is an idea as much a country. The idea of America is big enough to include people with all kinds of names and all kinds of faces."

James washed up and threw the water from the wash pan onto Mama's petunias by the porch. He wasn't sure he was a pacifist like Mama and Papa. Sometimes he wanted to punch some of the boys at school. He never had punched anybody, but he wasn't so sure that he wouldn't if they pushed him too far. He figured he would know about being a pacifist soon enough. A few of the boys had been pushing pretty hard lately. Maybe he'd punch them out. He felt like it.

Little Maggie, now almost a year old, held out her arms to James, expecting to be lifted into her high chair. He held her up high until she squealed with laughter, before setting her down in the chair.

"I don't think we have to worry about being singled out as German spies," said Papa. "We both grew up here. Folk know us."

"Did you read that article about the family over in Indiana?" asked Mama. "They were a German family accused of spying." She set a platter of hot pancakes on the table. "A mob showed up on their doorstep and searched their house. They found two barrels of sauerkraut and one of pickles. They thought that was proof enough that they are German sympathizers." Mama shook her head and sighed. "It sounds like some kind of joke, but they were serious. Doesn't that beat all?"

"I skip over that claptrap when I read the paper," scoffed Papa. "Did they think the family was sending messages to the Kaiser hidden in pickles?"

James couldn't help laughing. Maggie laughed, too, clapping her little hands.

"Your Mama's right, James. We have to take all this mass hysteria seriously." Papa helped himself to a stack of pancakes, passing the platter to James. "We aren't German citizens. We're Americans whose families came from Germany. Towns and cities across America are made up of folk like us who came from other countries. Most of us came because we wanted to. Some of us came because we were made to come as slaves. But we're all in it together. This country belongs to all of us. Unfortunately, when people get scared, they forget. When they forget, they can do some pretty stupid, foolhardy things. Now lets bless this good food before it gets cold." He said a simple prayer of thanks and James tucked in.

"Can you say the preamble to the Constitution?" asked Mama. She had been helping him prepare for a civics test at school.

"Yes," said James, reciting, "'We the People of the United States, in Order to form a more perfect Union...'"

Baby Maggie sat in her high chair stuffing pancakes into her mouth with both hands. As James began reciting she began babbling along with him. He ignored her, trying not to get distracted, "...establish, Justice, insure domestic Tranquility, provide for the common defense, promote the general Welfare. . ."

"Mmmm, doo le da, ba ba ma ba mmm," Maggie's voice grew louder and louder.

"and secure the Blessings of Liberty to ourselves and our Posterity, do ordain and establish this Constitution for the United States of America.' There, I have it!" James exclaimed. "I think you know it, too, Maggie."

She reached out to him with syrupy hands, "Ames!" she called. It was her version of James, one of her first words.

"Those are more than just words," said Papa. "Our Constitution and Bill of Rights protect our freedom."

"Yes sir." James had heard it all before. He hoped Papa wouldn't go into a long speech about freedom of thought and speech, the way he did sometimes.

"What about the names of the states and their capitals?" asked Mama, wiping syrup from Maggie's hands and face.

"I've studied those until I can just about say them in my sleep," said James.

"Good, then you'll do well on your test," said Papa. "You'd better be off before you're late."

Picking up his books and lunch, James said, "I'd better be off before Claude Higgins and his gang, that's for sure."

"Don't let those boys get under your skin, James," said Papa. "They're just itching for a fight. It won't matter much one way or another what you do. They'll be on you for it. People like that just want somebody to beat up on. You're smart to stay out of their way."

"I wish it were that easy," said James, waving goodbye. He headed out for the two-mile walk to school, hoping that he hadn't cut it too close. Claude had been held back at school twice. He was bigger than any of the other boys. He was almost as big as the teacher. The last thing he wanted was to run into Claude Higgins.

Chapter 2

TROUBLES

When James got off to an early start, he loved the walk to school, even in bad weather. To the unfamiliar eye, the land seemed flat. But gentle rolling hills were cut through with tree-lined canyons and creeks. There was always something to see. He surprised an occasional jackrabbit, sending it bounding away. More often than not, cottontail rabbits stopped their grazing and froze in place. They seemed to think that if they stayed still enough, he couldn't see them. He always pretended he couldn't, so as not to hurt their feelings. Once in a while he saw coyotes at play along the ridge of the deep, red-banked canyon that marked the half-way point between home and school. It was usually too late in the morning for deer, but sometimes he saw one gracefully bounding through the prairie grass.

In the summer when he had a day to himself, James liked to follow the canyon, taking Old Shep with him. He skipped rocks on the creek, and explored pools where bass hid near the bottom and water bugs skated on the surface. A mile or two away, the creek was joined by another that marked the border between the Matthias property and their neighbors.

When he got across the canyon bridge and started up the hill on the other side, he could see Patricia Bates. Her daddy, Hank Bates, stood waiting with her by their driveway. Mr. Bates owned the mill on the edge of town. Their place was a little over a mile from the Matthias farm. A private road led up to their big house on the side of the hill looking out over the canyon. Patsy was six-years-old and too young to walk to school by herself. James stopped every morning and took her with him.

"Mornin' James," said Mr. Bates. "How's your folk?" It was the usual greeting. Then he added, "That Claude Higgins and the two Taylor boys was just along—no more than ten minutes ago. Little early for them. Patsy says they like to pick on you. Hope they aren't makin' fun of you for walkin' her to school. We sure do appreciate it."

"No, I don't reckon that's it," said James "My Papa says it wouldn't make much difference what I do or don't do. They're just itching for a fight."

"I'll tell you what," said Mr. Bates. "You stand up to 'em. Somebody needs to clean that

Claude Higgins' plough for him. He's gettin' too big for his own britches."

"I'm not looking for a fight," said James. "Besides Jess and Frank Taylor would be on me like ducks on a June bug if I lit into Claude."

"You've got a point there, Son," said Mr. Bates. "But with a bully, you got to call their bluff. Choose your time. Then don't be afraid to let him have it. You may not be able to best him, but you can make it hurt so much he won't want to do it again. Sometimes you have to meet force with force. It's like I tell the Missus, President Wilson needs to quit mealy-mouthin' and tell that German Kaiser to put up or shut up. Course I know your folk don't hold with fightin'. Mrs. Bates don't either. But that's my opinion." Giving his little girl a pat on the head, he said, "Well, off you go."

Patsy began a stream of chatter that usually lasted all the way to school. She noticed every bug and butterfly. She found it hard to pass up a dandelion blossom or seedpod. She usually picked up enough rocks along the way to pave a road. He had no idea what she did with them. But they were important to her, so he didn't fuss about it.

As he watched Patsy he wondered if his sister from before was alive. *Does she collect rocks, too? What became of her? What became of our parents?*

They soon reached the top of the hill where the land leveled out. They could see nearly all the way to school.

The road ran along parallel to a lane lined with sand plum bushes where Gerald Hill ran his cows out to pasture. Where the lane turned, leaving the road, there was a thick grove of sumac bushes. Claude Higgins was waiting for him on the other side. Frank Taylor flanked him on one side and Jess on the other.

"Well lookie who's on his way to school," said Claude. "If it ain't that fancy pants Matthias boy. Thinks he's a big shot."

"You mean that orphan somebody dropped on the church steps?" sneered Frank.

"Yeah, 'cause nobody wanted him," snickered Jess.

"Except the teacher," said Frank. "Teacher's pet! Thinks he's smarter than everybody else."

"Mornin'," said James, trying to keep his voice even. He didn't want to frighten Patsy. Claude and the Taylor boys fell in behind them. James usually managed to avoid them by leaving earlier. When they did catch him on the way to school, they usually followed with a string of taunts. This morning, they didn't say anything. Instead they kept a steady stream of pebbles aimed at his back. It wasn't enough to hurt, just enough to irritate him.

Patsy took ahold of his hand. Her eyes were big as saucers.

"What's the matter, orphan? Too chicken to stand up for yerself?" Claude jeered. He threw a pebble that missed, hitting Patsy on the ear. She cried out, probably as much in fear as from pain. They were almost at school. James could see other children up ahead.

"Run Patsy," he said, "those big girls will help you." Whipping around he confronted the boys. "You had no call to do that to Patsy. If you want to pick on me that's one thing. But leave Patsy alone."

"Yeah? Or what?" sneered Frank.

"You'll be in trouble with Hank and Norma Jean Bates, for one thing," said James.

"Gonna tell on us like a sissy?" mocked Jess.

"Big talk," said Frank. "He ain't gonna do nothin'. He's a scaredy-cat."

James turned his back on them and walked on, relieved to see Patsy had reached the older girls up ahead. Suddenly Jess and Frank jumped him from behind.

They held him. "Take that, you yellow-bellied coward," said Claude giving him a hard punch in the stomach.

James doubled over in pain. But he didn't try to fight back. He couldn't have if he'd wanted to. How can you fight back when your arms are pinned behind you? The Taylor boys let go and ran. All three boys were gone before he could catch his breath.

James got to school just as Miss More rang the bell by the door. "Are you alright, James?" she asked.

"Yes ma'am," said James. He knew he ought to tell her, but he was afraid it would just create more trouble. So he said no more.

"Are you sure?" She looked at him, worried. "I saw Patsy. She'll be okay."

Theirs was a two-room school right on the edge of the town. A sign above the door read, "Sage, Oklahoma Public School." The day began with morning meeting in a large common room. At the front of the room were rows of desks anchored to the floor. The seat of each desk was joined to the front of the desk behind ending with the desk at the front. The seats folded up to make it easier to sweep the floor. Patsy sat in one of these desks with the younger girls, holding a wet cloth on her ear. At the back were rows of wooden chairs where the older children sat now and where the grown-ups sat when the common room was used for community meetings and social events. Claude, Jess, and Frank sat in wooden chairs as far back as they could get, leering at James as he took a seat.

One of the younger children held the flag. Everyone stood, reciting, "I pledge allegiance to my Flag and the Republic for which it stands, one nation, indivisible, with liberty and justice for all." Then they sang "My Country Tis of Thee." After that, Mr. Tipton, who taught the older children, made announcements. Everyone stood again as groups were dismissed to their rooms.

As the younger children left with Miss More, everybody else got into line in the wide aisle between the anchored desks and movable chairs. Boys got in one line, girls in the other.

Frank gave James a hard shove in the back. Catching him off guard, it sent him reeling into Amos Counts, who was ahead of him. Amos fell into the chairs, knocking them out of place. "Watch what you're doin'!" he yelled, shoving James again as he got up.

James landed flat on the floor in the middle of the line of girls. The girls jumped out of the way, squealing. The boy's line looked like a row of dominoes going over. Amos lost his balance when he shoved James and fell into Earl Davis, who fell into Billy May. Billy, making the most of a good thing, deliberately fell into Jake Hill, who shoved Danny Smith, who shoved the chairs, sending half a dozen more of them to the floor with a loud crash. James was the only one of the boys who actually ended up on the floor. But chairs were everywhere.

"Whatcha tryin' to do over there in the girls' line, James," called Jess, "look at their underwear?" James could feel the red creeping into his face as he picked himself up.

The boys snickered and the girls turned on him like it was his fault. "Settle down, boys and girls," said Mr. Tipton firmly. "Let's get these chairs put back in place." James brushed himself off, face burning with embarrassment.

Several hours later, as school was ending, Mr. Tipton announced the results of their civics test. "Congratulations to James who made top marks." The class broke into applause, except for Claude and the Taylor boys. When he handed out papers, Mr. Tipton asked James to stay after school for a minute. As soon as the schoolroom cleared, Miss More came in with Patsy.

"James, we know that you are being bullied," said Mr. Tipton. "I'm afraid that not telling and trying to ignore the problem isn't going to make it go away. Today, Patsy narrowly missed being seriously hurt. You did a brave thing by sending her on and facing Claude, Frank, and Jess. But letting them punch you and not telling isn't going to solve the problem."

"Yes sir," said James. It wasn't like he'd let them punch him, but he didn't say so.

"Some of the other children saw what happened and reported it," said Miss More. "We know what happened."

Mr. Tipton looked at him sternly. "I want you to tell your parents and to tell Mr. and Mrs. Bates about this. We cannot allow it to go on. I'm going to have a word with some parents. I will not tolerate bullying."

"There are a lot of people who will tell you to fight back," said Miss More. "I don't think it helps most of the time. I know your parents wouldn't approve. But there are some things you can do besides fight. Ignoring the other boys isn't working. How about trying another strategy?" They gave him some ideas.

James wasn't so sure anything would work, but he agreed it was worth a try. Just about anything was worth a try.

He started home with Patsy, keeping a watch out for the boys. He was pretty sure they wouldn't do anything until he dropped her off, but he wanted to be ready. *I'll probably get my face smashed in before I get home*, he thought.

Chapter 3

HOLED UP

Ruby Swathmore lay gazing up at the ceiling of the Alabaster Cavern where she and her twin brother, Junior, were holed up. *Gettin' danged lazy*, she thought. It had to be well after dawn. The bats were back. The network of caves around the cavern was filled with them. Thankfully, there weren't very many in the Crystal Room where they'd set up headquarters.

She sat up, aching all over. "You ever get tired of hidin' out?" She looked over at Junior, who was still curled up in his bedroll like a caterpillar in its cocoon.

"Huh?" Junior stuck his head out of the cocoon.

"I said, you ever get tired of holin' up like this?"

"Well, reckon it's better'n jail," Junior yawned, rolling over.

Ruby and Junior Swathmore were two of the meanest outlaws to terrorize Oklahoma Territory. There were pictures of them in post offices and train stations from Dodge City, Kansas to Abilene, Texas that read, "Wanted Dead or Alive for Murder and Bank Robbery." They looked and sounded like a couple of big stupids. Maybe that is how they got away with what they did. But, anyone foolish enough to take them for stupid did so at their own peril.

Things weren't going their way at the moment. They were holed up after a string of unsuccessful robberies. The law had come too close for comfort.

"I been thinkin'," said Ruby.

"Hold it!" Junior sat up again, putting his hand out to stop her. "You start thinkin' and it means trouble. Every time."

"I ain't foolin'. I been thinkin'. Ever since we left St. Louis, I've been thinkin' about stayin' in that there hotel where we stayed. It weren't,... *wasn't* half bad," mused Ruby. "Never thought I'd want a bath more'n oncet a year, but after I got used to the shock of it, sittin' in that big bathtub felt right good. Couple of times a year might be real nice. Sure beat the wash tub Pa made us scrub down in every spring when we was kids."

"Yep," said Junior, yawning.

"It's the bed I'm thinkin' of most. The floor of this here cave is terrible hard. Reckon what it'd be like havin' your own bed with sheets and everything. Let's face it, Junior, we ain't as young as we used to be. We can't carry on like this forever. I'm hurtin' all over."

"You ain't goin' respectable on me?" asked Junior suspiciously.

"Now don't go getting' on your high horse. I didn't say respectable. I just said maybe we should ought to find another line of work."

"Well heck, we ain't finished robbin' all the banks from here to California like we set out to do," said Junior, disappointment ringing in his voice.

"That was just a bunch of rubbish that Genie Lady planted in your mind," scoffed Ruby.

"Weren't neither. Thought of it myself." Junior sounded highly offended. "Celeste was mighty pretty, but she weren't no genie."

Celeste was the woman they worked for a few years before. It started when they found a black alabaster box in the Crystal Room. The alabaster box was empty except for an image of Celeste's face that appeared when anyone opened the box. That's why Junior and Ruby thought she was a genie. Celeste hired them to find the wooden box that should have been inside. She said it was a family heirloom that had been stolen, but the truth is it held something that she wanted for her own evil purposes. There was more to Celeste than either Ruby or Junior realized.

"Sure you did, Junior. Thought of it all by yourself," snorted Ruby. "If that lady weren't, wasn't a genie, she was somethin' mighty suspicious. Knew how to get her way. That's fer sure."

"Yep," said Junior, flopping back onto his bedroll.

Ruby laid a change of clothing plus a dress, bonnet, and change of underwear on top of her blankets. She didn't wear the dress that often, only when she wanted to go unrecognized. Her bedroll was the closest thing she had to a suitcase and she liked to keep it ready to go at a moment's notice. She carefully rolled everything up, making sure it all fit just so. Sitting on it, she said, "As I was considerin' our options this mornin', that wooden box came to mind."

"Considerin' our options?" Junior sat up again, incredulous. "When did you start usin' highfalutin words like that? Wasn't, weren't. You sound like Celeste or that German Count she was married to."

"Reckon it don't hurt," said Ruby. "We's a gonna have to quit soundin' like ignorant hicks if we plan to do anything but hide out from the law the rest of our lives. Folks judge you by your language. I heard Celeste say that. She was talkin' about us as if we was, *were* worthless trash. I reckon she wasn't just blowin' off steam." She sighed, almost wistfully. "I'm startin' small, 'weren't' and 'wasn't'. Figure I can work my way up. Wouldn't hurt you, neither."

"Hoity toity," Junior ridiculed.

"Like I was about to say," said Ruby, ignoring him, "I don't buy that family heirloom hogwash she tried to feed us. She wanted us to hunt down Grace Willis because she was after that box. She never said how come Grace Willis had the box. There must be somethin' mighty big in it. 'Member how she went off her nut first time we saw her?"

"Yeah," said Junior. "We was standin' right up there." He pointed to a large black alabaster rock that stood on the other side of the room, across the river that cut its way through the cavern. We opened that black box thinkin' maybe it was full of gold. There weren't nothin' in it but her face looking at us from the lid."

"You don't call that bein' a Genie Lady or somethin'?" Ruby asked. Not allowing him to get a word in, she plowed on. "She thought we oughta be dead. She thought some magic was protectin' that box so as if somebody opened it she'd have 'em. When she found out the box was empty, she couldn't get here fast enough. Now I ask you, who's gonna make a fuss like that over somethin' from their family? We ain't stupid."

"What you gettin' at, Ruby?" Junior asked. He was fully awake now. "Celeste ain't no genie. It took her durned near a week to get here after we found the box. Ain't no genie in the world gonna be takin' the train from California if they's lost a treasure. A genuine genie'd be here lickety-split on their magic carpet." He paused a moment, letting the magnitude of this statement settle in. "But if you talkin' magic—and I don't deny it was mighty fishy seein' her face in that box—but if that's what you're talkin' about, I don't want no part of it. Too dangerous. I'd rather face a posse of every federal marshal between here and St. Louis than fool with magic." With that Junior climbed out of his bedroll.

"Yeah, but maybe she was callin' our bluff," said Ruby, taking the other side of the argument. "Maybe she was just sayin' she could do stuff to us when she couldn't."

"That don't explain her eyes lookin' at us when we opened that black alabaster box," said Junior skeptically.

"Maybe it was like a telegram," Ruby suggested. "If they can send words all the way from Dodge City to Chicago, maybe they can send faces."

"Where'd you come up with a dumb notion like that? 'Bout as stupid as anything I ever heard. Ain't nobody what can send pictures through the air," Junior scoffed. "Anyways, she said there was a wooden box that was supposed to be inside. She was goin' on about another box inside that one, too. If they was both wooden boxes, they woulda burnt when we blew up that house."

"You got a point there, Junior," said Ruby, shaking her head. "But the bottom fact is our reserves is gettin' low. I'm tired of shinnin' around every post office and train station 'cause our picture is up for the whole world to gawk at—and it ain't even a good picture. The way I figure, that wooden box wasn't in the house when it burnt. We seen that bunch of half-wits she sent out there to sift through the ashes. They didn't find nothin'. If the box was full of gold or diamonds or somethin' like that, wouldn't they of found 'em? That kind a stuff don't burn up. That's why we followed 'em, wasn't it? So we'd get our cut? That's why I reckon it wasn't there. We get our hands on that box, we could live in one of those fancy hotels if we had a mind."

"How in tarnation do you think you gonna find the wooden box?" Junior asked indignantly. "Go back to Celeste? She threw us out."

"Celeste was after Grace Willis. Reckon Grace knows," said Ruby.

"Then you shouldn't ought to of shot her," said Junior.

"Reckon I did shoot her," sighed Ruby. "Just like you shot that namby-pamby husband of hers. 'Bout the dumbest thing we ever done."

Chapter 3

"Well heck, we was employed," said Junior, picking up his hat and planting it on his stringy head of hair. "We was supposed to shoot 'em."

Chapter 4

AMBUSHED

Mrs. Bates always met James and Patsy at the driveway. She was already coming for Patsy before they got there. Patsy ran to meet her, blurting out how she was hit by a rock, crying as she told the story. "I was starting to worry," Mrs. Bates said, arms around Patsy. James told her what had happened and how he'd been asked to stay for a few minutes after school.

She gave Patsy a reassuring kiss on the ear. "It's about time somebody had a talk with their parents," she said. "I don't know about Claude's family. They rented that place last year. I don't know where they came from or anything about them. I don't think anybody else does either. They haven't really become a part of the community—I've invited them to things, I know Hank has too, he asks every time Mr. Higgins stops at the mill. But they don't seem to want to mix. Now I went to school with Sally Taylor. She'll have a fit when she learns what her boys are up to. They're good boys, or they will be when she holds their feet to the fire." She smiled knowingly at James.

When they got to the driveway gate, she paused. Patsy ran on ahead. "Hank thinks you ought to just have it out with Claude," she said, "give him a good thrashing. I don't know about that. Your daddy took a good bit of ribbing when he was in school. He was a grade ahead of me, you know. As far as I remember, he never fought anybody over it. My people didn't hold with fighting either. Anyway, the world ought to be big enough for people with different ideas about things." She sighed. Then giving him a pat on the arm she said, "You're a good boy, James. Thanks for standing up for Patsy."

James wasn't surprised to see Claude, Jess, and Frank up ahead waiting for him just on the other side of the bridge. *They think they had a big a victory on the way to school. They won't let it rest now,* he thought. Getting top marks on his test hadn't helped, either. Claude didn't care anything about schoolwork, but Frank and Jess did. It rankled them when James got first place in anything. He was pretty sure they planned to jump him and beat him up this time for sure.

They hadn't seen him. Hoping they'd give up and go on home if he waited long enough,

James darted behind a stand of sunflowers along the road near the bridge. Hunkering down, he waited. They didn't seem to be in a hurry. His legs were cramped, but he didn't dare move. If they found him hiding out, it would go even worse for him.

Then he remembered. It was one of those flashes from before that came to him at unexpected times. The picture in his mind was so vivid it felt like it was just happening.

He is huddled under brush and trees, waiting and listening. His little sister is next to him, her face buried against his chest. His father and mother are there, too, hunkered down, arms around them both. Daddy, Mamma. That's what he called them. He can't see their faces, but he knows it's them. Daddy has an arm over Old Shep; he's there, too. He can see his Daddy's hand clearly, a big, firm hand. There are footsteps coming close. A man pauses—so close they can hear him breathing. They hardly dare to breath. A woman calls out, "Come on Junior. They's long gone by now. We can't afford to lose any more time. Reckon we'll have to find 'em the hard way. We've got some serious trackin' to do." The footsteps walk away.

The memory vanished, leaving James sweating. Through the sunflowers, he could see the boys, still on the other side of the bridge waiting for him. He decided to get it over with, wondering if it was time to try the new strategies. *Can't hurt,* he thought. *Might hold them off until one of the neighbors comes along on the way home from town.* It was a scant hope and he knew it.

Waiting until the boys were looking the other way, he stepped back onto the road. *Catch them off guard,* he mentally rehearsed Miss More's instructions. He walked briskly towards them, trying to act carefree. "Hi. I was expectin' you," he said before they could jump him. He tried to sound cheerful. He didn't feel cheerful. He was scared, really scared.

The boys were a bit taken aback, but only for a moment. "Here's the big sissy," said Jess. "Stayed after school to tell on us. You dirty tattle-tale."

Mr. Tipton said not to be afraid to report. *They need to know you aren't going to just take it,* he reminded himself. "Mr. Tipton asked me what happened this mornin'," said James, trying to stay calm. "I told him the truth. He already knew what happened anyway."

"Yeah? And what was that?" sneered Frank.

Claude stayed back. He said nothing, standing there, arms crossed, just waiting.

"That you two held me while Claude gave me a punch in the stomach," said James. He looked for an escape. If he could bolt free, he was faster than any of them. Mr. Tipton said running away from an uneven fight was not cowardly. But they had him hemmed in on three sides.

Jess and Frank jumped him, as expected. They pinned his arms back. "You good for nothin' tattletale," said Claude, holding up his fists, ready to punch.

Face your tormentor, Miss Moore had told him. *Try to keep bullying from being satisfying.* "So what are you gonna get out of punchin' me?" asked James. His tried to sound untroubled, but he could feel his heart thumping. "Anybody can punch somebody who's bein' held down. I'm just curious why you'd wanna bother."

"I'll take you one on one any time you name," sneered Claude. "Let 'em go."

Frank and Jess released him.

"That didn't answer my question," said James, brushing his arms off. He fought to keep his voice from quavering.

"Seein' you beaten to a pulp is what he gets out of it," said Frank.

"Yeah, give it to him Claude," Jess egged him on. "Make him bleed."

"You lily-livered coward, 'fraid to fight, ain't cha?" taunted Claude.

Miss More told him to refuse to take an insult and just agree with the bully. "I probably am," said James. "You're bigger'en me, Claude. I don't like gettin' hurt. I can't figure why you want to hit somebody smaller than you when they don't hit back. Doesn't make any sense to me."

"Quit your jawin'," said Frank.

"Go on, give it to him Claude!" said Jess, practically dancing in excitement.

James kept his eyes on Claude, "Reckon y'all ought to know that Mrs. Bates is fed up with Patsy bein' afraid on the way to school. She's goanna have a talk with your mother."

Frank and Jess looked at each other. "Says you," said Frank. But they quit taunting him and dropped back. James stood his ground.

Claude stood there looking at him for a minute. He took a swing.

James braced himself. It took every ounce of courage that he had, but he didn't flinch.

Claude checked his punch so it fell just short of hitting him in the jaw. "You're nothin' but a yellow-bellied Kraut. You ain't worth the trouble it'd take to squash you," Claude said. Turning, he followed Jess and Frank, who had already started for home.

James let out a sigh of relief. He was pretty sure Claude would try again, but at least he hadn't punched him this time. He was pretty sure, too, that Frank and Jess would leave him alone. Just knowing their mother would find out put the fear into them.

He started for home. That was when he realized that his trousers were soaked. He'd been that scared.

Old Shep usually met him at the driveway that led to the house and barnyard. But just as he started up the hill toward the drive, he saw Old Shep coming. "I was in trouble back there," he said, patting Old Shep on the head. Old Shep seemed to understand.

When he got home he had to change clothes. It wasn't easy to tell Papa, especially about wetting his pants.

"I expect it was a pretty scary situation, Son," said Papa. "You're probably right, too. He'll try again. I have a feeling Claude's got a burr in his saddle about Germans."

"But why would he call me a Kraut?" asked James.

"Oh, it comes from German immigrants liking to make sauerkraut," Papa said. "Other people like it, too, but it is just one more way to make us look different. Sounds like you handled it real well, though. Mr. Higgins has some straw for sale. I've been meaning to go see him about it. Might be able to get in a helpful word while I'm at it."

James wasn't so sure. It could just make Claude more determined to smash him. But he didn't say anything.

That night after he went to bed, James thought about the memory of hiding. It was one more unconnected piece in his big puzzle. He could feel the fear creeping over him again. It wasn't fear of Claude, either. It was something else that happened long ago. *I wonder why they were looking for us? Who were they?* He shivered and pulled the covers over his head.

After Mr. Tipton and Mrs. Bates had a talk with the Taylors, Frank and Jess quit walking to school with Claude. They weren't friendly with him, but at least it broke up the gang.

Papa went to see Mr. Higgins about hay and came back empty handed. He didn't say much about what happened; only that Mr. Tipton had been there before him. Later, James heard him tell Mama that Mr. Higgins flat out refused to sell to a Hun. James knew that 'Hun' was another name used to make fun of German-American families. "It may explain why the boy has it in for James," Papa said.

"They're new to this area. Nobody from around here has that attitude about German-Americans," said Mama. "I wonder if they've had some bad experiences where they lived before?"

"Possibly, but I doubt it," said Papa. "There are a lot of folk who are on the lookout for somebody to hate. Reckon Higgins is one of those. If he weren't after German-Americans he'd be after somebody else. No wonder the boy acts like he does."

"Oh dear," said Mama. "Poor James."

Right, thought James. P*oor James is in for a pounding.*

Chapter 5

BIG RED

"That calf of yours is looking good," said Papa one evening, as they were finishing chores. "I think you should exhibit him at the county fair. You can start getting him ready if you like. First thing will be to train him to walk with a lead."

James had been caring for the calf, Big Red, since it was only a few weeks old. He'd taught it to drink milk from a bucket by letting it suck his fingers and gradually worked it up to eating grain mash mixed with milk. Big Red was a real pet.

With Papa's coaching, he began to work the calf over the next few weeks. Getting a halter on him was the easy part. Big Red wasn't afraid of being handled. He loved to be scratched behind the ears. So the halter went on without any trouble. Getting him to go where James wanted was another matter entirely. The first thing Big Red did was push one side up against the barn. He wouldn't budge. Then he tried lying down and refusing to get up. "Just be patient," said Papa. "He'll come around."

Working with Big Red helped James keep his mind off of school. He made sure he got off early enough every morning to avoid Claude. Mr. Tipton's watchful eye prevented anything too serious on the playground. Claude never missed an opportunity to taunt James on the playground if he thought Mr. Tipton wasn't looking, though. He was full of dirty tricks.

James learned to look before he sat down and never to put his hand in his desk without looking first. One time there was a big blob of molasses on his chair. He narrowly missed sitting in it. He regularly found tacks. Somebody was just waiting for him to forget and sit without looking first. Once there was a snake in his desk. He opened his desk another time to find that somebody had emptied a whole jar of spiders inside. They were crawling everywhere. James didn't need anybody to tell him who was behind it. He tried not to react. *Don't rise to the bait*, he told himself. It was a relief when school came to an end.

Over the next few weeks James was busy with his regular chores, the wheat harvest—always a big event in early summer—and teaching Big

Red how to walk with a lead. Big Red seemed to be getting the idea and no longer bucked his head, jammed himself up against the barn, or laid down in the middle of training.

Once wheat harvest was over, Papa taught him how to groom Big Red. Big Red loved getting a rub. But teaching him to stand still for grooming was not so easy. "Give him time," Papa advised. "Don't reward him by rubbing when he moves around. Make him work for it by standing still for you. Start rubbing. The minute he moves, stop. When he stops, give him the rub."

By the time the county fair opened, James had not only taught Big Red how to walk on a lead and stand still for grooming, but had him getting in out of a trailer without balking. He'd even learned to tolerate having his hooves wiped off. Big Red and James worked together like a team, even at bath time. When he was groomed, Big Red's white face and red-brown coat gleamed.

Claude Higgins was exhibiting a calf, too. It was a fine-looking Shorthorn. Like James, he spent most of the day in the livestock exhibit barn once the fair opened. The barn was full of boys like them, watching their calves and cleaning out pens every day. James tried to be friendly. Claude's pen was in another lane of the big exhibit barn. He was cleaning his calf's pen when James stopped by right after the fair opened. "That's a mighty fine lookin' calf, Claude," said James. "Good luck."

Claude didn't say anything. He didn't even look at him. But when James walked on, he said in a loud voice, "There ought to be a law again' Huns showin' at the fair." James knew it was for the benefit of the boys around him.

There was only one girl showing a calf, Alvera Weeks. She was from a neighboring town. Her big brother Buddy was showing, too. Buddy was with her most of the time. The afternoon of judging for the older group of exhibitors, Buddy was gone. The exhibit barn was nearly empty because almost everybody wanted to see the judging. James missed it because he fell asleep in Big Red's pen and didn't wake up until after everyone else had gone.

He awoke suddenly. He was puzzling over what awoke him so abruptly when he heard the sound of footsteps stealthily slipping past. Listening, he felt fear rising within. It was the old fear; fear left over from the long-ago memory of hiding out from an unknown attacker, somebody called Junior.

A scream from just down the aisle brought him back to the present. It was Alvera Weeks.

Somebody laughed. "Scared ya, didn't I?" it was Claude's voice.

"Leave me alone," said Alvera.

James jumped out of Big Red's pen without opening the gate. Claude had pushed Alvera to the ground and was standing over her jeering.

"Ain't got big brother here for protection, have ya? Shouldn't let girls exhibit. Ain't right. Why dontcha take that calf and go home where you belong."

"Leave her alone," said James.

"Says who?" Sneering, Claude turned on him.

"I say so," replied James, trying to keep his voice calm.

"Think you're big enough to make me?"

"No," said James. "But you'll have to beat me up first. By then Alvera and I will make enough racket to get you kicked out of the show. Is that what you want?"

Claude looked at him with pure hatred in his eyes. "Dirty Hun," he said. Then he spit right in James' face. James didn't flinch. It was all he could do to keep from lighting into Claude. But he didn't. He thought about what Papa would do. He looked Claude right in the eye as he took his red bandanna out of his back pocket and wiped the spit off his cheek. Then he carefully folded his bandanna and put it back in his pocket, still looking at Claude.

"If you ain't the biggest sissy I ever met," said Claude.

"You'd better get out of here before Buddy gets back or he'll knock the beans out of you," said Alvera. "He's bigger'n you and you know it."

"There'll be no knocking anybody down," said James, surprised at how calm he felt. "It wouldn't do any good, would it, Claude. Something's buggin' you and it doesn't have anything to do with me or Alvera."

Claude turned on his heel and walked away.

"That was really brave, James!" Alvera exclaimed. "I thought he was going to knock you down for sure."

"No, it wasn't brave," James admitted. He felt like his knees were going to buckle. "I just don't believe in fighting." For the first time, he knew he was a pacifist, too.

"Then we'd better not tell my brother or he'll clean that boy's plow for sure," said Alvera.

"Are you okay?" asked James. "I need to go wash my face."

"Yeah, I reckon you do!" Alvera grinned. She said she was fine, but James figured she was probably a bit shaky, too.

James and Alvera walked out to the pump where he washed his face. He was shaking all over. But he hadn't wet his pants. *I guess that's progress.* He almost laughed aloud at the thought of it.

The next afternoon was the judging for exhibitors in his age group. He gave Big Red a bath first thing in the morning. There was an area just outside the exhibit hall with a large water tank and windmill. It was set up especially to provide water for the livestock and as a place to groom them. Alvera and Buddy were already there. Alvera was giving her calf, Sassy, a good scrub. When it was his turn, James rubbed Big Red down and gave him a thorough rinsing, wiping his hooves until they were shining. When his thick coat had been combed through, Big Red looked like a winner.

Later in the morning, Mama and Papa came bringing baby Maggie. "Ames!" called Maggie, reaching out her arms to him. He let her pat Big Red. Then he held her hand while she walked unsteadily, leading them around to see the other calves that were in the competition. When they got to Alvera's pen, she got to pat Sassy. Sassy was perfectly groomed.

They were about half way up the next aisle, when Maggie broke free and ran ahead. They laughed as she rocked back and forth like a ship at sea in her effort to stay upright. Without warning, she turned and began trying to climb up the gate to Claude's pen. "Maggie! No! You can't go up there," called James, running after her as fast as he could.

Suddenly it felt like he was moving in slow motion, living something all over again. His other sister, little Gracie, was climbing up a ladder and he was calling, "No! You can't go up there." Then he was back in the present, pulling a squirming, squealing Maggie from the gate she was determined to climb.

James' heart was racing. His hands trembled. "She's fine, James," said Mama. "Little children do that. Sometimes they want to try things before they're ready."

"Claude isn't here anyway," said Papa. James knew they thought that was why he had the shakes. But it wasn't. It was something else, something he couldn't quite put together.

Fortunately, Claude's calf didn't seem to be perturbed by all the excitement. It nosed at their fingers as they reached through the pen to pat it. It had been well groomed. Its coat glistened.

"That's a nice-looking calf, James. He'll give Bed Red a run for his money," said Papa. "He's been treated well, too. You can tell by how he reacts to people. I'm glad to know that about Claude."

When they returned to Big Red's pen, the gate stood open. Big Red was missing. James called to Alvera, but she'd been sitting in Sassy's pen reading a book since they left her. She hadn't seen anything.

Frantic, James ran up and down the aisles. He found Big Red at last, wandering outside the exhibit hall covered with mud. "Oh James, you must have failed to shut the pen properly," said Mama. "How could he have gotten so dirty? What are we going to do?"

"We're going to give Big Red the fastest bath in history," said Papa, reaching for the bucket James kept in the stall. "Come on Son, we'll have to be quick. You have less than an hour before judging starts and Big Red will have to be dry."

"Papa, I shut that pen," said James when they were out of earshot. He didn't want to worry Mama. "Somebody let him out."

"I know, Son," said Papa. "I didn't expect mischief. In hindsight, I realize we shouldn't have let you leave the stall this close to judging. Now don't go jumping to conclusions. It could have been anybody."

Everybody had finished grooming much earlier, so the grooming area by the stock tank was free when they got there. "I think the rules say you have to do this yourself," said Papa, "but there isn't anything in the rules that says I can't hand you the water!"

As he began washing Big Red down, it was clear that mud had been thrown on him. Fortunately, it hadn't caked. They were able to get Big Red rinsed off in record time. Having Papa to keep buckets of water coming from the tank helped.

Alvera went up and down their aisle asking. Nobody had seen anyone lurking around the pens. James couldn't believe any of his fellow competitors would have done such a thing, even Claude Higgins. Everybody around was helpful. Not only did they furnish extra buckets so Papa could keep the water coming when James washed Big Red down, but they brought extra rags so James could get Big Red rubbed dry. By the time judging began, James led a dry, perfectly groomed calf out into the arena. They won first prize, too, and the chance to go to the State Fair in Oklahoma City. Alvera won a red ribbon.

"Big Red's ribbon is partly yours, Alvera," said James. "Yours and everybody in our aisle. They all helped get him ready."

Claude won a blue ribbon, too. But when James congratulated him, Claude cut him cold. "Don't mean nothin' anyway," he said.

It wasn't until he climbed into bed that night that James had time to think about things. He wondered why his first sister, little Gracie, was climbing up a ladder. *Children do that,* he thought. But why had it left him feeling so shaken?

Sometimes he felt as if there was some kind of magic at work—bad magic—keeping him from remembering. When he felt that way he reminded himself that he didn't actually believe in magic.

Chapter 6

AN UNPLEASANT DISCOVERY

"Somethin's eatin' you, Ruby," said Junior. "Has been ever since we left St. Louis. Threw your timin' off, too." They were in the midst of an argument that had been going on for several days.

"You blamin' me for all those banks that bested us?" Ruby's temper flared.

"Now hold your horses, Ruby. I ain't sayin' it was all your fault. But you haveta admit, you ain't been at your best. I figured a good rest and you'd be back ta form. But your timin's still off. You gotta get a grip. We got us a future. They's banks where folk never heard of us just waitin' for us, so as they can hand over their gold."

"Junior, sometimes you're so dumb you'd ride your horse across a river to get him a drink 'a water," said Ruby, thoroughly disgusted.

"Let's think about this here situation sensibly," she continued. "Here's the bottom facts: Fact Number 1: we ain't as young as we useta be. Fact Number 2: the competition is gettin' tough. Ever since the Dalton Brothers and the Youngers moved into Oklahoma Territory. . ."

"The Dalton Brothers specialize in robbin' trains," Junior interrupted. "I hear there's good money in it. Might join up with 'em if it comes to it. They could use a gunslinger like you and somebody with my brains and good looks. I ain't so bad with a gun either. That's a lot of talent for one man to carry around with him."

"Don't interrupt me," said Ruby. "The Daltons is fools. They been grandstandin' like the law was a buncha idiots. They all started out as lawmen. They think they know all the tricks. They's been robbin' banks, too. Not just railroads. They ain't above rustlin' horses and cattle either—'specially the Younger Brothers. Just gets the law nervous and sets 'em on edge. Folk like us pay fer it. I don't have a mind to join up with any of that bunch or any other bunch of outlaws. Working that deal with Celeste done burned me. I ain't joinin' up with nobody."

"You're forgettin' Frank Dalton," Junior interrupted again. "He was a Deputy US Marshal.

Kept the boys on the straight and narrow till he was killed trackin' down horse thieves."

Ignoring him, Ruby barely paused for breath. "Big shots like the Daltons don't have no respect for women, neither. I'm better'n the lot of 'em, smarter, too. I can out shoot anybody—I admit my timin' has been off lately, but it's comin' back. Don't matter how good I am, that don't keep folk from showing disrespect." Ruby was really worked up now.

"Well heck, Ruby. No denyin' you bein' a women. Bottom fact is women don't do important stuff." He dodged the boot she threw at him and ducked as the other sailed past. "Anyways, when Celeste showed up here at our cavern with the Count and those gunslingers lookin' for the black alabaster box, they was plenty respectful." said Junior.

"No they wasn't," Ruby contradicted. "You could see it in their eyes. It was like they was sayin' that a woman had no business out-shootin' 'em. I could tell. Except for the Count. He was respectful. Those gunslingers thought I should oughta be sittin' in some shack wipin' snot noses and cookin' 'possum stew for a bunch of brats. I ain't puttin' up with that kind of disrespect."

She shook her finger at Junior. "That's not even my main point. The world is changin' Junior. We need us a pile of gold to live off whilst we figure out what to do next. I'm not of a mind to die in a gun battle. That's where we're headed, plain as the nose on yore ugly face. And I ain't interested in show business—a bunch of people gawking while I shoot holes in stuff. That ain't for me. So what else can we do?"

"Come on, Ruby," said Junior. "We've had us some real good times."

"Yeah, but think of all the work we done and how little we got to show fer it? We don't have enough gold stashed away here to see the year out. I get a bit of gold put aside and next thing I know you've done gone and spent it on a fancy saddle with silver do-dads or some durn fool thing."

"Gall dang," said Junior. "You take the fun out of ever'thing."

"Junior, we gotta think about what next. What can we do besides theivin'? That's why I was thinkin' along the lines of that box. We gotta have us some capital. See, I figure she's got gold in there. They was a lot of gold hauled out of California back in Gold Rush days, nuggets bigger 'n a man's fist. Maybe its gold nuggets she's got in it. A box full of those and we'd be set for life."

Junior shook his head in disbelief. "I ain't havin' nothin' more to do with that Genie Lady. She and her magic are trouble."

"Course, it could be diamonds," Ruby said dreamily. "Uppity folk like Celeste like all that sparkly stuff. Emeralds, rubies, sapphires, all them jewels like was in Aladdin's cave. People pays a lotta gold for stuff like that. Shoot, it won't matter if it's gold or jewels. Course jewels ain't as easy to get rid of as gold." She sighed. "We'd go out to California like Pa said when we was kids. Heck, they live like kings and queens out there. We could live in one of them fancy hotels and have strawberry shortcake and lemonade for breakfast every mornin' if we was a mind to."

"Ain't gonna go into farmin' neither, too much work," said Junior ignoring Ruby's reverie.

Ruby snapped back into reality. "You're good with numbers, Junior. You can do sums in your head 'bout as fast as I can shoot. You could learn to read."

"No. I ain't learnin' to read." Junior was emphatic. "That's final. Man's gotta draw the line somewheres."

"Ain't that hard," Ruby said. "Shucks, I been learnin' myself to read studyin' the 'Wanted' signs in the Post Office. Gotta know what's bein' said 'bout us. How else you reckon I'd a knowed all the stuff I knows about the Daltons? Couldn't go up introducin' myself to the Post Master sayin', 'Good afternoon, Your Officiousness, would y'all be so kind as to read that there wanted poster? I'd like to see if they's givin' a fair report of our criminal activity.'"

Junior rolled his eyes.

The argument continued for the rest of the day and off and on through the next week. They were still holed up. Their last attempt at robbery was at a bank in Garden City. A woman at the bank recognized them from the last time they were there. They barely got away with fifty dollars and a lawman on their tail to boot. They ditched him somewhere along the Cimarron River. It was too close to their hideout for comfort, so they had to lie low for a while. Again. It was starting to become a pattern.

They took to exploring the vast network of caves surrounding the Alabaster Cavern. It was something to do and Junior said they'd better have a plan up their sleeve in case they were ever cornered in the canyon near their hideout.

Ruby thought having some alternatives was a good idea, but she wasn't keen on the Bat Caves that were laced through the hills and canyons surrounding the Alabaster Cavern. "I ain't havin' no bat gettin' in my hair and makin' it fall out."

"Shoot," said Junior, "We'd use the cave at night whilst the bats is gone and we'd be gone in the day robbin' banks whilst they was sleepin'."

Ruby was practical. Sometimes Junior made good sense. She didn't buy his argument about being off robbing banks or about the bats. But bats or no bats, the idea of alternatives made sense. The trail of unsuccessful robberies they'd left on their way back from St. Louis had her troubled. Even more troubling was their recent pattern of bad luck. A few years ago, robbing banks was child's play. It was getting harder. She was losing interest in it, too.

Exploring the area was no easy challenge. They had to hike over white gypsum bluffs that were covered with patches of buffalo grass, sage-brush, and weeds. It was interlaced with loose rock and red, sandy dirt. One minute footing was secure, the next minute it was like stepping off into nothing but space or taking the fast way to the bottom of a canyon on a landslide.

They found that it was easier to locate the opening to the Bat Caves if they watched in the evening. That's when the bats began flying.

Just about sunset, a ribbon of black started to drift up out of nowhere. Hundreds, thousands of bats poured out. Once they saw a ribbon, they moved toward it until they had an idea of where it was coming from. They'd quickly make a mental note of the spot, noticing distinctive fea-tures like a cluster of gnarled trees or a partic-ular growth of sagebrush or sumac. Their work was complicated by the fact that ribbons of bats seemed to float out of multiple entrances almost at the same time. The air was full of bats coming from more places than they could count. The next day they'd return to locate the entrance they'd spotted and have a look at the cave. It wasn't smart to try to explore in the dark. The footing was too treacherous at night.

It was on one of these exploring excursions that they made a discovery that put an end to their argument over futures. It drove all thought of the wooden box and the possibility of gold or jewels from Ruby's mind, too.

They started early on foot one morning, making their way through brush and prairie grass, over protruding gypsum rocks, and around gnarled cedar trees. They'd identified three locations earlier in the week. Two had already been explored and disqualified before the sun was well up. Junior had high criteria. The cave entrance had to be obscure. There had to be hidden shelter for their horses not far away, but not so close as to give away the entrance to the cave. There had to be a water supply inside. Ruby agreed and insisted that they also needed a natural escape for smoke when they built a fire. Smoke bellowing out of a cave entrance would be a dead give-away. "I ain't sleepin' no place where you can't build a fire," she said.

They were both savvy scouts. Even on these outings, they left the ground they'd covered looking as if nobody had ever been there.

All of a sudden, Junior, who was slightly ahead of Ruby, flattened himself on the ground, signaling for her to do the same.

He didn't have to explain. She trusted him. If he signaled a halt, she halted. He'd have done the same. It was one of the keys to their past success in escaping the law. Ruby dropped to the ground instantly, cautiously pulling herself up even with Junior. Just ahead of them, hemmed in by a thick grove of cedars, half a dozen splendid horses were tethered. Junior studied the situation from behind a scrawny patch of sagebrush that clung to the gypsum bluff. "We'll wait it out," he whispered as Ruby crept up alongside.

Neither of them was interested in stealing the horses. It wasn't even up for discussion. Getting rid of them was too risky when you were as well-known as they were. They knew that eventually somebody would come for the horses. After about an hour, Junior whispered, "If they ain't showed up before sunset, reckon we'd best be back here before dawn. I don't cotton to campin' out here all night with the rattlesnakes. Besides, nobody's gonna try to leave the canyon after dark."

"Yep," said Ruby grimly. "Best know who our new neighbors are. Reckon it's the law onto us?"

Chapter 7

MORE TROUBLES

It promised to be a beautiful summer day. When James got up, the sky was the bluest of blues. Maggie was already in her high chair calling, "Ames! Ames!" when he and Papa returned from doing morning chores.

"It is such a lovely day, James," said Mama as she set out scrambled eggs and a big platter of hash browns. "Soon as the separating is done and the milk buckets washed out, we're going to town. Do you want to come with us to buy school clothes or would you like to have the day to yourself?"

Town meant Cedar Hills, the large market town about twelve miles away. Cedar Hills was much larger than Sage. Along Main Street there was a department store, a movie theater, dime store, drug store, and an ice cream parlor with a soda fountain—that was just one side of Main Street. It was a hard choice. But James chose to have the day to himself. Mama said he could explore along the creek until time to bring in the cows. "If you like, I'll pack you a lunch."

"I like goin' to town, but maybe I'll stay. I can pack my own lunch, Mama."

Mama frowned at him. "'Going', James. You know I don't like you dropping your g's."

"Yes ma'am," he said. It was like playing to two audiences. Mama and Papa expected him to speak nice, crisp English. It probably came from being immigrant children whose parents had to learn the language. Just about everybody else talked in a bit more relaxed way. He already stood out at school. Talking differently just made it worse.

Thankfully, Papa changed the subject. "There won't be many more days like this before school starts, Son. I can't blame you for wanting to be out enjoying it. If I could get away with it, I'd join you and we'd do some fishing. We are going to have to take Old Shep with us, though. We'll need him to watch the wagon when we're in the shops."

"You'll have to trust me to pick out your school clothes, James," said Mama. "You are growing so fast, sometimes I think you've outgrown your new clothes before I can get them home."

Long before noon, James was exploring pools beside the creek bank along their property. He came to the wide pool that gathered to create a little waterfall just before the creek took a plunge downward. Below the falls it continued its winding way along the northern border of the Matthias farm and off into the canyon. It was the perfect swimming hole and one of Papa's favorite fishing holes. Gathering some small pebbles, James began skipping them across.

Suddenly he felt a prickly feeling on the back of his neck. He wasn't alone. Whipping around he came face to face with Claude Higgins and some boys he knew from school, Earl Davis, Jake Hill, Danny Smith, Amos Counts, and Billy May.

Except for Claude, they'd all been friends until this year. James wasn't sure what happened. It was partly due to the fact that Amos Counts and Claude both had coon dogs. Sometimes they went coon hunting on weekend nights. You could hear the dogs baying up and down the other side of the creek. Papa wouldn't hear to coon hunting. He said it was cruel. A raccoon didn't have a fair chance with dogs after him. "That's claptrap," said Amos. "Where'd you get a dumb fool idea like that? Coons is smart enough to drown a dog. Takes more'en one dog to stand up to a coon."

It was all James could do to restrain himself when Amos called Papa's opinion claptrap and dumb. He wanted to give him a swift punch in the stomach. Maybe he wasn't a pacifist after all. The only thing holding him back was what Papa would say.

It was more than coon hunting that set James apart. The boys also sided with Claude on the war. The United States hadn't decided on going to war, but the boys had. They didn't want to be friends with anybody who didn't agree with them. Papa could say all he wanted to about democracy and the importance of different viewpoints. It didn't matter to the boys. Their way was the only way. Sometimes it was hard being different.

Remembering Miss More's advice, James went on the offensive. "Y'all are good. You really snuck up on me. Couldn't of done better if you were Indian scouts."

The compliment was lost on Claude. "Lookie here, if it ain't the yellow-bellied Kraut all by his-self. You're a chicken-livered, traitor."

"I'm as American as you are," said James, trying to stay calm.

"You ain't American, you're a German," said Amos. "If you was an American, you'd stand up for your country."

"There's lots of ways to stand up for your country besides goin' to war," said James. His mind was racing ahead, trying to figure out how to distract them long enough to get away.

"I reckon we ought to throw this good for nothin' in the creek," sneered Claude. "That'd be one less Kraut."

"Good idea! Let's throw 'em in the creek," said Jake.

"Yeah, but he's got his clothes on," said Danny. "We wouldn't wanna get those nice clothes wet."

"Can Germans swim?" snickered Billy.

"One way to find out," said Amos. "If we throw him in and he drowns we'll know he was a traitor."

"Yeah, and if we throw him in and he doesn't drown we'll know he's a traitor," said Billy, laughing at his own joke.

Earl hung back. James tried to make eye contact with him, but Earl looked down. He knew he couldn't talk his way out of this. He'd have to make a run for it. His best bet was to jump in the creek and escape on the other side before they could follow. In the instant James hesitated, thinking it over, they were on him, pinning him down, stripping off his clothes. He went limp, trying to make it as unrewarding as possible. Even so he lost some buttons from his shirt and was scratched up pretty badly. "Coward!" Claude gave him a kick, rolling him over on his stomach to pull his shirt off.

"Stop it!" said Earl. "You've got no call to treat anybody that way. It ain't right."

"Poor baby," said Claude, ignoring Earl. "Better give the baby a bath."

They carried him to the creek and threw him in. James was glad to be in the water. At least he had a chance. He swam to the other side under water, staying under until he had to come up for breath. The boys were waiting with rocks. "Get him when he comes up!" yelled Danny. "That'll teach him a lesson."

"Hey, y'all. Give him a chance," yelled Earl. "You could hurt him."

"That's the idea, stupid," said Amos.

"Whose side you on anyway, Davis?" yelled Claude.

"Five to one ain't fair. It's downright mean," said Earl, backing away from the others.

"Get on outta here before we throw you in, too," said Claude, hurling a rock at him. Earl dodged.

"I'm tellin,'" he yelled, running away as fast as he could. In the moment the boys were distracted by Earl, James crawled up on the opposite bank where he was out of range. He was out of breath, stripped down to his under shorts, and barefoot, but he knew he could outrun them. He knew this part of the creek just as well as they did, maybe better. He'd cross over upstream and cut back through to the barn. They wouldn't follow him there.

Claude picked up his pants. Taunting him, he threw them as high as he could into a tree. The others began throwing until his clothes and shoes were scattered beyond reach. "You look like a plucked chicken!" yelled Amos.

"Yeah, brock, brock, a-brock!" called Jake. Putting his thumbs under his armpits, he flapped his arms, squawking at the top of his voice. "He won't get far without his clothes on. Got all his feathers plucked off!"

"That's a good idea. We ought to tar and feather the chicken," said Claude. "His folks has gone into town. Jake you and Danny Smith follow him. Amos, me and Billy will cut through and catch him before he gets back to their barn. That's where he's headed."

James wasn't sure what would have happened next, if a man hadn't appeared on horseback. "Having fun, boys?" he asked.

"Yeah, what's it to you?" asked Claude. Amos, Jake, Billy, and Danny cowered behind Claude.

"I just met Earl Davis. I don't like to see a fight that's rigged, either," said the man calmly. "Doesn't seem right, does it?"

"I say it's none of your business," said Claude, standing tall. He'd grown at least six inches since the end of school and stood tall as a man.

"I've just made it my business," said the man pleasantly, looking down at the boys. "Now I think you'd better get James' clothes for him, don't you?"

"Get 'em yourself," said Claude. With that, he turned and began walking away. Before he'd taken no more than half a dozen steps, he fell to the ground, a lariat rope around his middle. The other boys froze with fright.

"Pick up the boy's clothes," the man politely asked again. "Amos, your father would never approve this kind of behavior. Neither would yours, Billy. Jake, Danny, you boys are better than this. Seems like Earl Davis was the only one of you man enough to walk away. Now get the boy's clothes for him." With that he dismounted, standing over Claude, who was still on the ground.

"Sorry to knock the wind out of you, Son," he said kindly. "I don't hold with back talk to your elders. Somebody has been treating you real bad for you to want to do such a mean and cowardly thing to that boy. I can't think of any way you can make it right. Best thing you can do is get on home. Don't ever let me hear of you bullying James or anybody else again."

The man reached down and pulled Claude to his feet. He didn't say anything as Claude walked away. Once he was out of range of the rope, Claude turned and spat on the ground.

The other boys scrambled to find James' clothes. It took some doing, too. His trousers were high up on a tree branch. Amos, who was the best climber, crawled out as far as he could on a limb and the others handed him a long stick. Meanwhile, the man pulled a blanket from his horse's back. There was no saddle. He rode bareback.

Walking up to the pool, he dropped it on the bank. "Dry yourself off, James, and get dressed. These boys have something to say to you."

James swam back across the creek and shook himself off. Grateful for the blanket, he waited for his clothes. When he was finally dressed, the man made the boys look James in the eye directly and apologize, one by one. "Now boys, I need to have a private word with James. Go on home. Let's make this the end of it. Loyalty to your country is a matter of the heart. It doesn't have anything to do with what country your ancestors came from."

"Thank you, sir," said James, when the boys were gone.

"Don't you know who I am, Son?" asked the man.

"No sir," said James.

"Then I think it's about time you did," said the man.

Chapter 8

A VOICE FROM THE PAST

The man sat down on a large rock next to the creek. "Where's Old Shep?"

"He went into town with my folks," said James, still baffled. He wasn't afraid, just puzzled. The man wasn't the sort who made you feel afraid.

"I've known you from the time you were born," said the man. "I promised your Mamma and Daddy that I'd look after you if anything ever happened to them. But it seems to me that Karl and Hannalore Matthias are doing a pretty good job. They are fine people, James."

"You're Mr. Nichols." It came to him in a flash. "I rode with you on Song of the Wind once." James paused for a long time, searching for the rest of the memory, but it wasn't there, only the names, Mr. Nichols, Song of the Wind.

Mr. Nichols didn't rush him. After awhile he said, "Yes, James. You knew me before."

He was almost afraid to ask, but he had to know. "Did they leave me on the church steps? My mother and father?"

"No, I did," said Mr. Nichols, motioning for him to sit down next to him on the rock. "I'm so sorry, James, but your parents died. You had no family to care for you. I knew that Karl and Hannalore wanted a family and you wanted a home. Seemed like a good match."

"Why can't I remember?" James asked numbly. "And why didn't you take me to Mama and Papa Matthias and tell them all about me if you knew? What if I hadn't been found?"

He felt tears welling up all of a sudden. He didn't want them to, but he couldn't help himself. Somewhere in the back of his mind, he'd always hoped that he would find his birth parents one day, that he'd know who he was. He wiped away tears that had begun to spill down has face using the back of his hand, but they just kept coming. Mr. Nichols gave him a big pocket-handkerchief.

Leaning down, James crossed his arms on his knees, burying his face in his arms. He cried. It was like he'd been waiting to cry all this time. He cried like he had never cried before. His whole body cried. His heart cried. He cried until he was empty of tears. But he wasn't empty of sadness.

Mr. Nichols waited. "Sometimes not remembering is a good thing, James," he said gently. "It was a Sunday morning when I left you. Karl and Hannalore were getting ready to go to church. You didn't have long to wait. I knew you would be safe. And you had Old Shep. It was better for you not to remember then. It was better for me not to be there. Nobody needed to know about before. It wouldn't have helped. In fact, it could have done some real harm."

"I had a baby sister named Grace. Did she die, too?"

"No, but she lives far away from here. She's in a very good place, too, the right place for her. One day soon we will go see her." Mr. Nichols said. "You need to get re-acquainted with your sister."

"She tried to climb a ladder," said James. "She wasn't supposed to. Something terrible was going to happen. And we were hiding from somebody. What was it? Why were we hiding?"

"Maybe we should start at the beginning," said Mr. Nichols, putting his arm around James. "I can't promise that it will make a lot of sense. Shall we start with your parents?"

James nodded his head yes.

"Your parents were David and Grace Henry. Your father was a geologist and cartographer—he made maps."

"He made the map for me?"

"No, your mother made the map just for you. She was a schoolteacher and very good artist. After they got married your parents went west to help map the land beyond the Rockies all the way to the Pacific Ocean."

"Is that how I got the abalone shell?" James wondered.

"No, that comes later in the story. After you and Gracie were born, they returned to St. Louis and the Willis family home. So you were living in St. Louis when Gracie climbed the ladder."

"That's why Mamma and Daddy died?"

"Yes and no. It was what your sister Gracie found in the attic that led to their death." Mr. Nichols then told James how his mother's family went west on the Santa Fe Trail, how his mother was kidnapped and taken into Oklahoma Territory with Old Shep as her only comfort, and how she escaped."

"Old Shep?" asked James. "It couldn't be the same Old Shep. He isn't that old."

"Old Shep is no ordinary dog," Mr. Nichols smiled kindly. He explained why they came to be in the Alabaster Cavern and how Grace Willis broke the spell that held the Last Crystal in a black alabaster box. "There are some things only a child can do, James."

"I don't understand," said James. "What is the Last Crystal and how did it get in the black alabaster box?"

"I remember trying to explain it to your Mother. It isn't that easy without going on and on. But I shall try," said Mr. Nichols. He thought for a moment before beginning, "Long ago, when the Earth was fresh and new, Immortals lovingly tended it like a garden. But, as the Earth grew older, the time of the Immortals was passing. Mortals came. The Immortals feared that Mortals would not treasure the Earth. So they set aside seven crystals. Each one held water fresh from the dawn of Time. "Water of a Thousand Lights," we called it, rich, life-renewing water to heal and repair the world when it was misused. It was given to Immortal Twins, Celeste and C'lestin, born the day the Earth was made, to care for the crystals and to decide when Mother Earth needed them. At first, the twins used their powers to do great good. But Celeste, the firstborn, became distracted by the ways of mortals. She longed to be the most beautiful woman on Earth. She stole the crystals, binding them to herself with the darkest of dark magic. She was very, very powerful then. But there was a price to be paid in exchange for the dark magic. She had to give up her immortality. When she became mortal, she lost all of her magical powers except for those binding the crystals. These remained, for she wove them into the spell that gave her power over the crystals. One by one she has used the crystals to stay young and beautiful. Now only one remains, the Last Crystal. It is nested in a golden box within a wooden box—both of the boxes were hidden in the black alabaster box in the Alabaster Cavern.

"When your mother opened the alabaster box, it was just the beginning. There was more magic to unravel before the boxes within could be opened and the crystal freed. The crystal was, in some strange way, bound to her. She could keep the crystal safely as long as she didn't open the boxes."

"I remember now," said James. "We were playing on the ladder. It was a fold-down ladder to the attic. I wasn't supposed to play with it, but I did anyway. You could pull on this cord and the ladder came down. Then you could climb up a few stairs and jump down. It was so much fun! It always made Mamma angry because we were never, ever to go up into the attic. I never did, but I disobeyed her. I couldn't resist playing on that ladder. Then Gracie started up the ladder and she wouldn't come down. I was afraid she would fall. That's when she saw the awful lady in the box and we had to leave the house in St. Louis."

James shook his head in disbelief. "I must not be remembering it right. That doesn't make sense. A lady in the box? I thought I heard them talking. It must have been Gracie's imagination—and mine."

"It doesn't make sense unless you allow for the magic," said Mr. Nichols. "It was part of the magic, still is. If you open the wooden box, Celeste's face appears—the lady who took the crystal. She can see you from the box. As to the last box, the golden one that holds the crystal, I cannot say for sure what would happen, though I have my suspicions. That spell has yet to be broken. Fortunately, Gracie didn't open the golden box."

"I followed Mamma up the ladder. Gracie went to sleep and she wouldn't wake up. Mamma asked me to put the boxes back in a carpetbag. She said she couldn't be in charge of the crystal anymore. You came right after that."

"I did," said Mr. Nichols.

"And you said Gracie couldn't be allowed near the boxes or the lady, ever again. We kept moving. Sometimes we had to hide out. I remember hiding at the edge of a woods, behind some thickets, but that memory isn't very clear. Who were we hiding from?"

"Tell you what," said Mr. Nichols. "I was coming to see if you would like to go into Sage for tea. Miss More has invited us. There are some things she can tell you about before, too."

"You know Miss More?" It was almost too much to take in at once. James felt as if an explosion was going on inside his head.

Mr. Nichols nodded and smiled.

"But I have to be back in time to bring in the cows."

"I think we can arrange that. It's been a long time since you rode on Song of the Wind. Hop on behind me."

Hopping on wasn't so easy. Mr. Nichols had to reach down and give him a hand.

Chapter 9

MISS MORE AND HER BROTHER

Sage was a small town made up of pretty little wooden houses and a few stores. The school sat on the west end of town, surrounded by a large yard and grounds. It marked the beginning of the main street that ran west to east through town. But a fenced-in pasture separated the school from the town proper. So it didn't feel like the town really began until you got to Bates Mill on the south side of Main Street. Next to the mill was Hitch and Wagon, a harness and wagon outfit. Hitch and Wagon was a long building that looked like a barn, surrounded by a yard where wagons were left for repair. James liked the smell of leather from all the saddles and the harness gear inside. Papa said they used to sell wagons, but people went to Cedar Hills to buy wagons now. Most people repaired their own wagons, too, except for work on the iron parts that required the blacksmith.

Counts Blacksmith was directly across the road from the mill on the north side of Main Street. The blacksmith was Amos Counts' uncle. His grandpa still worked there most days. Next to that was an abandoned building that had once housed a tinsmith. On the other side of the tinsmith building was May's Oil Delivery. You could buy kerosene for lamps, oil, and grease in the small store. Billy May's father picked up kerosene, oil, and grease at the railroad station in Cedar Hills in his three-tank wagon and made deliveries to farms around Sage. He kept his wagon parked in a barn in the back where he stabled his team of horses. Mr. May was especially proud of a brand new gas pump. There were only three families in all the Sage area who had cars, but Billy May's father said it was the wave of the future. He could repair just about anything that didn't require a blacksmith, too. Across the road from May's Oil Delivery and next to Hitch and Wagon on the south side of Main Street was the big icehouse where Papa bought blocks of ice to put in the top of the icebox that stood in their kitchen. Just past the icehouse Cottonwood Street cut across.

Further along on Main Street was MacLean General Store, on the north side. The MacLean girl was in James' grade at school. Papa and Mama usually bought groceries at MacLeans. Mama liked their selection of fabric in the dry goods section, too. The post office was next door, run by Inez Smith, Danny's great aunt. The bank stood next to the post office. A hardware store run by Danny Smith's family was directly opposite across the street. Two other streets cut across Main Street. After Cottonwood, if you were coming into Sage from the West, was Elm Street. Elm Street marked the end of the business section. It was flanked by a church on either side facing Main Street. Beyond Elm Street, was Oak Street. Houses with expansive yards and graceful trees filled in the rest of Main Street and lined both Elm and Oak streets and the side streets that cut through. Smaller houses with tiny garden plots and room for a cow and chickens were at either end of Elm and Oak Streets where the town gave way to farmland. It was a small town, more of a village. But nobody said 'village' in Sage. 'Village' sounded like something from Europe or New England.

Miss More lived on Oak Street at the far end of town, just off of Main Street. She had a tiny bungalow with a flower garden in front. A picket fence went all the way around the whole house. She had a carriage house in back. She didn't have room to keep a horse, though. She boarded her horse with the family who owned the farm across the road.

When they arrived at Miss More's house, James saw that a horse was hitched to a post in front by the fence. As they dismounted, Mr. Nichols told Song of the Wind to wait. He didn't tie him to the hitching post. James remembered that. Song of the Wind was never tied or tethered. He and Mr. Nichols seemed to understand each other.

Miss More came to the porch all smiles. "Do come in, James. There is somebody I'd like you to meet."

"I see Otis is here. Good," said Mr. Nichols, pausing on the porch.

There was hardly a boy or girl who went to Sage School who didn't know Miss More's front porch. In the summer, she usually spent early mornings and late afternoons in her garden. Children liked to walk past her house when she was gardening. She'd lean on the fence to have a chat. More often than not, a chat ended on her porch swing with cookies and lemonade. She was the sort of person who could listen to troubles and keep a secret. So at one time or another, just about everybody found their way to Miss More's porch, sometimes even grownups.

A man stood as they entered her tiny parlor. "Hello, James," he said, shaking James' hand. "I am very happy to see you again. I doubt you remember me."

"No Sir, I'm sorry," said James.

"This is my brother, Otis," said Miss More. "Come on into the kitchen. The tea is waiting. Some things are better with a cup of tea. James, shall I make you some teakettle tea?" Seeing his

77

puzzled look, she said, "Your mother liked tea-kettle tea. It is hot water with milk and sugar and sometimes just a touch of tea."

"Okay," he heard himself say. He felt as if he were in one of his memories, like he was watching himself.

"I'll bet you're wondering how we all know each other and you," said Mr. More, offering him a chair at the tiny kitchen table. He looked like an older version of his sister, kind, bright-eyed— almost mischievous, but taller and thinner. "It goes back to how you came to be on the steps of the church that morning."

Miss More hurried about pouring tea, making teakettle tea for James. Seating herself at the table at last, she began. "Mr. Nichols showed up on my porch one evening, late. You were with him." She looked at James intently. "You're remembering something, aren't you?"

Suddenly James felt himself nearly swept away by another flood of memories. He remembered the night Mr. Nichols came for him and for Gracie. His parents had just tucked them into bed. He remembered Mamma giving him a kiss and Daddy putting his big hand on his forehead. He remembered feeling loved. He remembered awakening later, with a start. Mr. Nichols was there, Gracie was with him. He helped them climb out the upstairs window to escape the fire that destroyed the house where they were living. And he remembered walking up the steps to Miss

More's house, not knowing her or where he was. Mr. Nichols had knocked on the door.

"Good evening. Are you looking for someone?" Miss More had asked. There was a puzzled look on her face.

"Sorry to trouble you so late, Miss More. I'm Mr. Nichols and this is James. Here, this will introduce us." He had reached into his jacket pocket and handed her an envelope.

"There was a letter," said James, suddenly returning to the present.

"Would you like to see it?" Miss More asked. "I have kept it in my Bible ever since."

James nodded his head yes. He couldn't find words.

"May I read it to you?" Miss More asked.

James nodded again.

She opened the envelope and read.

My dear Myrtle,

I admit that I hope you will never see this letter. It is to introduce my dear friend, Mr. Nichols. Please welcome him as you would welcome me. It is a long story. Mr. Nichols knows it better than I do. His coming will mean that neither David nor I are here to take care of the children. As you love me, shelter James and Gracie until Mr. Nichols can decide what

*is best. And above all, never let them forget
how very much David and I love them.*

Your dear friend,

Grace Willis Henry.

Miss More's eyes were filled with tears as
she finished reading. "Would you like to keep
the letter?"

James shook his head yes. He didn't cry. All
he could feel was wonder. How strange it was
after all this time. He took the letter, looking at
the perfectly straight rows of writing.

"Remember how I told you that I know what
it's like to be bullied?" Miss More asked gently.
"Our older brother and sister bullied Otis and
me terribly. Our parents didn't help. In fact, they
made it worse. They just weren't up to the job of
being parents. If it hadn't been for your mother,
Grace Willis, I don't know what would have
become of us."

"She showed us kindness when there was
very little of it to be had," said Mr. More. "Your
mamma was about your age then—younger,
maybe. We always thought she lived with us
because she didn't have any family. When we
grew up, we learned differently. Our parents kidnapped her, and worse. I am sorry to say they
were very cruel to her. Old Shep was with her
then. They ran away together."

"Our father threatened to shoot Old Shep," said Miss More. "Your mother was more afraid for the dog than for herself, I think. I'll never forget that day. We thought the world had just about come to an end when she left."

Suddenly James remembered. "Old Shep came on my birthday. Mamma was so glad to see him. She couldn't believe it. She said dogs don't live that long. He can't really be the same dog she had then, can he?"

Miss More nodded and smiled. "Don't be too sure. Old Shep is a pretty remarkable dog, isn't he, Mr. Nichols?"

"That he is," said Mr. Nichols. There was a twinkle in his eyes.

"We never forgot her," said Miss More. "She didn't forget us, either. Your mother saw that we got to go to school."

"She was clever about it, too," said Mr. More. "The teacher gave us money to take home at the end of each week. We got so much a day for every day we were there. Nobody ever knew where the money came from. When Pa tried to get the teacher to tell him, she said she didn't know either—and I'm pretty sure she didn't. Of course we never got to keep the money. Pa took it. But it meant that he saw to it that we were in school because he wanted the money."

"When it was time for high school, we left home," said Miss More. "Your Mamma and

Daddy paid for our room and board and for our books."

"That's when we changed our name from Swathmore to More," said Mr. More. "Our brother and sister had run away from home by then. I'm afraid they turned out badly. There wasn't much anybody could do for them."

"It wouldn't have done to have the same name," explained Miss More. "By the time we left for high school, Ruby and Junior were already famous outlaws. So we just dropped the first part of our family name."

"Junior?" The memory of hiding came back to James, full force.

"Yes, he was named for our Pa, Hiram George Swathmore," said Mr. More, misreading James' reaction.

James didn't know what to say. *Was he the Junior in the memory?*

"It grieves me to say that Celeste hired our brother and sister to hunt your family down," said Mr. More. He gave a great sigh. "They killed your parents before Mr. Nichols could rescue them. Thank God he was able to save you and your little sister."

"James, my first thought was that I could adopt you myself," said Miss More. "But Mr. Nichols said there was a family who needed you as much as you needed them. You had the crystal with you, in a carpetbag. We didn't think it was wise for you to take it with you then. So Otis lifted you up so you could put the carpetbag on a shelf in one of the closets. It has been close enough to you all these years since. Early the next morning Mr. Nichols took you to the church where you were sure to be found by Hannalore and Karl Matthias. Your Mama and Papa Matthias love you as their own. I knew that was the best plan the minute Mr. Nichols proposed it. You had a wonderful, loving family before. You have a wonderful, loving family now.

"I haven't moved the carpetbag since. There are some things only a child can do," Miss More added. "I'm afraid it falls to you to look after it."

"You may safely keep the crystal as long as you don't open the boxes inside that carpetbag that hold it," said Mr. Nichols, "That is, if you will agree to look after it."

It was a lot for James to take in all at once: learning about his birth parents, the Last Crystal, and Miss More's family. He didn't know what to say. So he said nothing.

"I am going to be leaving before the new school term to go live with Otis and his wife," Miss More added.

"My wife is a teacher, too," said Mr. More. "She started a very fine school on the Cherokee lands where she grew up. Now we need a new teacher."

"Otis and Leoti have invited me to join them," said Miss More. "I'm about ready to retire and this seems like a good next thing to do."

James felt his heart sink. Miss More had been a real friend to him ever since he first started school. Until now, he hadn't realized what a great friend she had been.

"This isn't good-bye," said Miss More "I'm keeping my house in Sage. I'll come back in the summer when school is out," she patted his hand. "After all, I have my garden to tend. Maybe Leoti will teach me the Cherokee alphabet. By then I can teach it to you."

Suddenly James knew what he wanted to do. "I will take care of the crystal. It is my responsibility."

"Do you think you can keep it safe, James?" asked Mr. Nichols.

"Yes," he said gravely.

"You must promise never to open the carpetbag that holds the boxes, no matter what happens, and never to tell anyone how to find it," Mr. Nichols said. "That's really all it requires. It is that simple and that hard."

"Why can't you use the crystal now? Couldn't it stop the war from happening?" asked James. "War hurts the earth."

"Even water from the Last Crystal won't heal the hearts of those set on evil," said Mr. Nichols, pushing his chair away from the table. "But its waters could bring freshness where the Earth is torn and spent. Let's get the crystal."

"But Mama and Papa aren't at home," said James.

"Don't worry," said Miss Moore. "I will speak to them myself. I'm giving you my rock collection, too. It isn't a large one, but there are some nice pieces. That is enough for them to know."

James took a sip of his teakettle tea. Suddenly the cookies looked really good, he realized he hadn't eaten a one. "Can I tell Mama and Papa about before?"

"Tell them what you remember," said Mr. Nichols. "But not about the crystal. They are better off not knowing. They can't tell what they don't know about."

Afterward, James stood on a chair in Miss More's bedroom and lifted the carpetbag from the top shelf in her closet. He was tall enough that he didn't need any help.

Mr. Nichols said, "When the time is right, I will come for it. If there ever comes a time when you think it is too hard to keep your promise, you must tell me."

They put the carpetbag at the back of the top shelf in James' closet behind the wooden cigar boxes that held his moth collection. He knew it would be safe there. Mama was glad for him to collect moths, but she said his collection gave her the heebie jeebies.

"How will I know where to find you, if I ever need you?" James asked.

"All you have to do is call for me," Mr. Nichols said.

"But we don't have a telephone," said James.

Mr. Nichols smiled at him. "Not that kind of call, just call out my name. I won't be so very far away. Or you can send Old Shep. He always knows how to find me."

"There is something else, sir," said James, suddenly feeling shy.

"What is that, James?"

"My birthday. Do you know when my birthday is?"

"Why yes," said Mr. Nichols. "September 19, 1903."

"But September 19 is my found day—the day Mama and Papa found me."

Mr. Nichols smiled. "So it is."

Chapter 10

RUBY AND JUNIOR RIDE AGAIN

Ruby and Junior lay on their stomachs watching. They'd been there behind the scrub brush all afternoon. It was about an hour before sunset when six men appeared from out of nowhere, about forty yards away. They were carrying saddles. Even though Junior and Ruby had marked the spot a few days ago, they weren't sure where the entrance to the bat cave actually was. Breathlessly, they watched as the men saddled their horses and led them out of the cedar enclosure, one by one. "Bob Dalton," whispered Ruby nodding toward the first of the men. "Seen his picture in the train station." Soon another man followed. "That's his brother Emmett. Dick Bradwell, Bill Powers—they's been ridin' with the Daltons." She paused until the last of the men came out, leading his horse.

"Grat Dalton. I'd know 'em anywheres. Their pictures is startin' to get plastered over ours."

Junior did a slow intake of breath as the men led their horses away from the bat caves.

"Grat Dalton was handcuffed to two marshal oncet and got away," said Ruby. "They was one on either side of him. Marshals was takin' him to Texas. He was facin' twenty years. Tough as beef jerky, Grat Dalton. Bob's ruthless, least that's what they say. Emmett's the youngest." They watched as the men mounted their horses and rode up out of the canyon.

"Didn't know that trail was there," said Junior.

"Don't reckon it's an actual trail. They was mountin' mighty close to the cave, if you ask me," Ruby said with disgust. "Wouldn't take a lawman with half his marbles to find 'em. They act like the law can't touch 'em. That's just plain stupid."

"Figure we'd better have a look at that cave before they get back," said Junior grimly. "If they's set up headquarters, we best be movin' on tonight. Wouldn't want to wake up with one of 'em standin' over me grinnin' and I don't fancy lettin' 'em have our horses."

"Reckon they's left anybody behind?" Ruby worried.

"Nah," said Junior. "Didn't have extra horses. That's bad practice, too. Should have a couple of spares. For outlaws who's supposed to be so gall danged smart, they looks pretty sloppy to me. Must not be comin' back."

"Could of left the horses in two locations," said Ruby. "They didn't have bedrolls or nothin'. Must be plannin' to stay."

"Could've stashed 'em anywheres," said Junior. "Maybe they was just sittin' it out today."

Stealthily, they approached the cave entrance. It wasn't hard to find. The Daltons hadn't bothered covering their tracks. Junior pointed to them in disgust. He didn't say anything, neither of them did. Ruby automatically moved around to the other side of the entrance so they could have two views of what they were in for.

In another hour or so the bats would start drifting out of the many entrances to the massive network of caves that covered nearly two hundred acres of land. Ruby wasn't best pleased with the idea of bats, but she cautiously crept inside, following Junior. They had to take advantage of all the daylight left. She had her pistols in hand. It wouldn't do to be surprised.

After a few feet of narrow tunnel, a wide vaulted room opened before them. It wasn't the brilliant Alabaster Cavern where they headquartered, but plenty comfortable and secure. It had the added advantage of light filtering in from somewhere near the top. Light was subdued, but they could clearly see the area. There seemed to be only one way in. Any fire would find its way out through the rocks, undetected. A stream ran through one side before disappearing underground. It met all the requirements they had for a hideout, except for the disadvantage of already being occupied—and by one of the most notorious outlaw gangs in history, at that.

The second they were inside, Junior flattened himself on one side of the entrance to the tunnel and Ruby on the other. Stealthily, they moved around the circumference of the cave, going in opposite directions. When it was clear that nobody was lurking behind boulders, they put away their guns.

"They's left behind a load of truck." Ruby pointed to a stack of canned beans and the bedrolls that were pushed to one side of the remnants of a fire. There were several torches that the outlaws had used to light the cave lying around on the floor. "Reckon they's plannin' on stayin' awhile." She kept her voice down. Even though the cave didn't appear to be occupied, they didn't take unnecessary chances. One of the men could return.

Junior struck up a fire with his flint stone. Taking up one of the torches, he whispered, "Hadn't been here more'n a day or two, judgin' by the empty cans and cigarette butts. Got themselves a stash of liquor, too. Can't make out much in the way of footprints. Rock's too hard. Looks like they done found themselves a new hideout. Reckon what else is put away here?"

"We'd best be quick and get the heck out of here," said Ruby. "They'll be back before dark if they's comin' back."

After a few minutes of poking around Junior came up with some newspapers. There were pictures of the Dalton Gang plastered all over the front page.

Meanwhile, Ruby wandered among the boulders along the other side of the wide room. She grinned, beckoning Junior. "Gimme a hand." Together they lifted a small trunk out from behind one of the boulders where they could have a better look.

Junior gave a silent whistle. "Spect it's locked. With an outfit like that you have 'ta keep stuff locked. Makes it hard for one of 'em to slip away with the loot."

It was locked. "Okay, Ruby, you cover the door. I'm fixin' to get rid of this lock. Looks like all I need to do is pry off the fittins, lock and all. Nothin' but pegs holdin' it to the trunk. Anybody comes back while I'm at it, they got us dead to rights. You best see that don't happen." He took out his hunting knife and began to pry the pegs that held the lock to the wood around it, separating it from the trunk.

Ruby waited on the alert by the door. She wanted to duck down with her arms over her head in case bats started flying out, but she figured it would be better to lose her hair than have her head shot off if the Daltons returned. She resolutely stood guard hoping her hat would protect her.

Junior knew what he was doing. It wasn't long before he lifted the lid open, the lock and latch still securely fastened. His face lit up. He waved a sheaf of federal bank notes at Ruby, motioning her to come over. There were stacks of notes and gold coins, more than they'd ever seen, even in their best days.

"Must be from that famous train robbery over in Lillietta," said Ruby. "Reckon we'd better help ourselves and high tail it out of here. Wouldn't want to ask Bob Dalton's permission."

"I call it rent money for usin' our caves," grinned Junior "What we gonna put this in? Best not to take more'n we can carry."

He got no argument from Ruby. She took a quick look around, finding a cornmeal sack that was about a quarter full. "Best not to dump it. A little cornmeal ain't gonna a hurt."

"Yep," said Junior, stuffing bills into the sack. "We'll take some of each—notes and gold. Be a bit harder to notice. Best leave this place looking like we found it, too. The longer it takes 'em to find out what we've been up to, the longer we keep our necks."

Nobody needed to tell either of them that the Daltons would be unforgiving. They'd already made a name for themselves, showing no hesitation to shoot anybody in their way.

Junior tapped the pegs back into the holes where they held the latch in place while Ruby made sure they hadn't left so much as a hair on the floor. Then they carefully returned the trunk to its place. Throwing the bag of money over his shoulder, Junior looked longingly at the bottles of liquor.

"You take one of them bottles and I'll shoot you, Junior," hissed Ruby. "That's a promise. You can't hold your liquor any better'n our Pa could. I can't have you gettin' roostered up whilst we's trying to make our getaway."

Junior reluctantly passed up the liquor. Putting out the torch, he replaced it before they groped their way back through fading light to the opening passage. The bats were beginning to fly out now, making competition for the narrow tunnel space awkward. Cringing, Ruby kept her head down.

The sun was already setting as they began to retrace their steps. "We's cuttin' it mighty close," whispered Ruby. They were well on their way when it began to get dark. Fortunately, it was a clear night. The moon shone brightly, giving more than enough light. It wouldn't have been easy to find their way, but they would have felt safer with a little less light.

Junior led the way. Despite the light, it was slow going. They had to be careful not to leave tracks. It was a relief when the bat cave was out of sight behind one of the hills. "You lead now, Ruby," said Junior. "I'll take up the rear."

"We got our work cut out," said Ruby when they finally got back to the Cavern.

"Yep, can't let the light of day catch us any-wheres near this canyon," Junior agreed.

"Thing is, those Dalton boys may be sloppy, but they's ruthless," said Ruby, shaking bat guano off of her hat. "Where you reckon we oughta head for?"

Junior stopped for a moment, shaking his hat and scratching his head before he replaced it. "Reckon they's headed north for the Santa Fe. That'd be their best bet for holdin' up a train. Ain't been no robberies along that stretch from LaJunta to Garden City. Somebody's in for a bad surprise. Reckon we oughta head south along the Cimarron, then due West to Amarillo. We can cut on up toward Denver oncet we hit Amarillo."

"Yeah, but we ain't spendin' a penny of this until we's way the heck out of here. Denver's too close. I don't cotton to a tangle with the Daltons or any of that bunch. They'll be lookin' for their money. Best way to advertise is to start spendin' big money."

"Now ain't the time to jaw about it," said Junior. "Let's leave this place like we was never here." They lit torches in the cavern so they had enough light to work, then swept over all signs of their campfire and cleared the area of foot-prints, using large stalks of broom weed. "What about all this canned stuff?" asked Junior. "We can't leave it here. Can of beans'd give away the whole store. Can't get very far haulin' it either."

"Can't dump it in the river; might float," said Ruby. "We'll lug it down to where the horses are and dump what we can't carry on the pack horses down the canyon. Brush'll cover it up," said Ruby. "Take us a couple of trips."

When they stepped back out of the Cavern, an unpleasant surprise awaited them. The cornmeal bag had leaked, leaving a thin line of cornmeal that showed clearly in the moonlight. "Dang," said Junior. "Must of caught it on a rock."

"Musta happened after I started to lead," said Ruby. "They'll sweep the hills lookin' for us. Won't take long to find our trail. Means we can't come back here, don't it."

"Nope, can't come back," said Junior. "No tellin' how long that thing's been leakin'. Not much cornmeal left."

Ruby said, "Sorry we can't come back. I reckon this here's the nearest to a home we've had all these years. You go get the horses. I'll give the place a last look and bring the bedrolls and put out the torches. Can't have 'em findin' the torches either. We better make this in one trip, seein' as we've rolled out the welcome carpet to our door."

Back in the cavern, Ruby picked up a piece of black alabaster, shoving it into her pocket. She kept thinking of Grace Willis back when they knew her, when they were all kids. She wasn't sure why. There was no time to linger and meditate on it. Hoisting up the bedrolls, she made her way out through the winding passages of the cavern. The moon was still bright, too bright. It flooded light into the entrance of the cavern. Once outside, she set the bedrolls down and retraced their steps up to where the natural animal trail they followed split, wiping away the cornmeal with her broom weed. It wouldn't deter the Daltons for long, but it might delay them. They'd have to search both branches of the trail once the cornmeal trail left off. With any luck that would slow them down.

"Can't do anything about the broken twigs around the entrance, but those coulda been made by deer," she told Junior when she caught up with him.

"Maybe the wind will take the rest of it. We best not be here to see," said Junior. He wasn't hopeful. He had already dumped the canned goods in the canyon and covered them up with brush, saddled the horses, and loaded their two extra horses with bulging packs. They carefully walked the horses the long way out of the canyon, guided by moonlight and sticking to areas where they left the least evidence of their passing. It was getting dangerously close to dawn when they reached the southernmost end of the canyon and set out across the prairie, riding south along the Cimarron. At first they rode from sheltered area to sheltered area, pulling the horses behind clusters of cedar or cottonwood trees and listening. There was no sign of the Daltons. It wasn't until well into the morning that they began to feel at ease.

"We ain't so far from the dugout," said Ruby. "Reckon it's still there? We could hole up there and get some rest."

Junior seemed to think it wasn't a bad idea. They made their way across smaller creeks, finding the place where their family had settled when they were children. It was nearly nightfall by this time. They watered the horses at the creek, rubbed them down, staked them, and left them to graze. The whole place had fallen into ruin. The shed was collapsed into a heap. They checked the dugout to make sure some varmint didn't occupy it. Then, with a bit of effort, they cleared out the entrance and went inside with all their belongings. They each had a can of cold beans and threw themselves down to sleep.

"Think we ought to drop down and take the southern loop of the Old Santa Fe Trail," said Junior the next morning. Dawn was just beginning to stretch across the sky. "Haven't worked that area, might find a bank or two along the way."

"No banks, Junior," said Ruby firmly. "Let's take a look at what we got."

They counted out the cornmeal-covered money, more than five thousand in paper and a little over five hundred in gold. "We'd best figure out how to stash this or we're live bait," said Junior.

"Be more sensible to make for Amarillo and take the train to California," said Ruby, dusting cornmeal off a stack of notes. "We could start over in California. Shoot, Junior. We've got enough money here to start a bank. You'd make a good banker, 'cept you'd have to learn to read. Nobody's gonna give their money to a banker who can't read."

"You mean folk would just give their money to me?" asked Junior. "Where's the fun in that?"

Ruby thought for a minute. "The fun is figuring out how to protect the money from the likes of us. Now that could be a lotta fun. It would take somebody pretty clever with a lot of nerve."

Chapter 11

THE STATE FAIR

School started in August, not long after the county fair. There was a new teacher for the younger children. Patsy said she was real nice. James still walked Patsy to school. He didn't have to worry about Claude, though. Claude's dad kept him out picking cotton. But Claude was back in school the week Mr. Tipton announced that James would be missing school during the State Fair in order to exhibit Big Red. Except for Claude, everyone clapped and wished him well, even the Taylor boys. Earl Davis told him he hoped Big Red won first place. Jake Hill, Danny Smith, Amos Counts, and Billy May didn't say anything. But at least they left him alone.

"Think you're a real big shot," Claude said when he had a chance. "You're nothin' but a dirty Hun. Won't even fight like a man." Claude didn't try to fight with him anymore, but he took every chance to say something about people who were too yellow to fight or about Germans. With all of the news about the war in the newspapers, it wasn't hard for Claude to stir up sympathy among some of the other children at school. They didn't seem to understand that James found the war news distressing, too.

Nobody dared say anything ugly to him in front of Mr. Tipton. "Everybody in this room's ancestors came from someplace else," Mr. Tipton said when he heard some mumbling on the playground.

The week of the fair was the most exciting time James could remember except for when he met Mr. Nichols and Otis More. Big Red made the hour-and-a-half trip to the city without incident. James brought a bedroll so he could sleep in Big Red's pen during the Fair. Most of the exhibitors were about his age. They, too, were prepared to stay day and night.

Mama, Papa, and baby Maggie looked around after Big Red was securely in his pen. Norma Jean Bates had a quilt on display. She won first prize at the County Fair, too. Mamma wanted to be sure to see it. Later, Papa and Maggie stayed with Big Red so James could see the exhibits, too.

Maggie was growing so fast. She walked everywhere now without falling over, but she still liked being picked up. She could talk up a storm, too. When they returned from having a look at the exhibits, they found her running up and down the aisle between the fenced in pens where the animals were kept. She didn't want to go home, even when Papa promised they would come back the day the judging was to occur. "Maggie stay with Ames and Big Red, Maggie stay with Ames and Big Red," she cried as Mama carried her away.

James was too busy keeping Big Red's stall clean and visiting with other youngsters who were exhibiters to be lonely. On the day judging was to take place, Big Red looked terrific. Mama and Papa arrived just in time for the judging. Maggie jumped up and down with delight. She agreed to go to the arena without a fuss when James promised he would wave at her. "Having somebody to wave at is very important to an exhibitor," he explained. "It helps us to feel encouraged." He gave her one of his big handkerchiefs. "Now be sure and wave it so I'll see you."

James was in the group of exhibitors who were between ten and fifteen-years-old. Everybody had family and friends in the stands rooting for them. There was a big horse show to follow, so the stands were packed. Breeders and prospective buyers from all over the southwest were already crowding in to make sure they had good seats for the events to follow.

James looked for his family among the sea of faces. At last he located them. Maggie was waving the handkerchief to catch his attention. He waved back. Once the judging started, he would not be able to wave. He had to stay focused on business.

Just as the judging was about to begin, a breathtakingly beautiful woman entered the stands on the arm of a man dressed in a smart, fashionable suit, wearing a white cowboy hat. It was impossible to miss them. Even the judges turned and looked. James noticed, but he didn't have time to stare. He was too intent on taking care of Big Red.

Once the judging began, all of the exhibitors walked around the arena, parading with their calves. The judges watched closely to see how well the calves obeyed, if they had a proper stride, and their over-all appearance. Then each exhibitor and calf stepped forward for judging. There were several judges. The judge interviewing James asked what he had learned about caring for and raising a calf. He wanted to know about Big Red's health, how he was fed, and where James kept him at home. Then he looked over Big Red carefully, all the way from his head down to his hooves. James had to turn him around so the judge could see from every angle. Big Red performed like a real trooper.

Then the over-judge came. All the calves stood in a row facing the judges. The judges chatted together and began pulling calves out of the line, repositioning them in order from right to left. James knew they were ranking for blue, red, and white ribbons. He held his breath as they came to Big Red.

"You're Matthias?" asked one of the judges. "That's a German name."

"Yes sir," said James.

"What does that have to do with it?" asked the over-judge.

"They'll let 'em go anywhere," muttered the first judge. "The boy has a mighty fine animal, but it pains me to see a Kraut come out ahead of the others."

"Leave your politics out of it," said the over-judge. "He's only a kid." The over-judge had James lead Big Red to the front of the line where several other calves now stood. When it was over, Big Red not only won a blue ribbon, but first prize and the chance to go up for the Best of Show award the next day. As the others took their calves back to the stalls, he proudly walked Big Red around the arena alone while everybody cheered. Mama, Papa and Maggie waved joyfully. Mr. and Mrs. Bates and Patsy were there too, waving and cheering. Even the beautiful lady waved and blew him a kiss.

It was a disappointing blow to find "Kraut" painted in yellow on the side of Big Red's pen when he returned to the exhibit barn. James tried to wash it off before Mama and Papa got there.

He didn't want to worry them, but they saw it anyway. The paint wouldn't come off.

Nobody in the exhibit barn near Big Red's pen had seen anything. They'd all been in the arena exhibiting, too. Papa insisted that they report it to one of the officials, who promised they'd paint over the letters immediately. Someone came and painted the side of the pen brown, covering the yellow paint. Even so, it left James with a sick feeling.

Judging for the Best of Show was to take place the next day. Papa said that James couldn't stay there overnight, not by himself after the painting incident. "Maybe Maggie and I can get a ride back home with Hank and Norma Jean Bates, Karl," said Mama. "Then you can stay with James. If she gets a blue ribbon they'll be back tomorrow. If not, you will just have to tell us all about what happens. They're judging the handwork right now. I promised to stop by, so we'd best hurry."

Chapter 12

OKLAHOMA STATE FAIR
1917 Sept. 22-29
Sept. 27
The Great Horse Show & Auction

CELESTE'S SURPRISE

Celeste looked in the mirror and smiled at what she saw. *I am the most beautiful woman who has ever lived.*

Being married to a wealthy Texas rancher suited her nicely. She especially liked the fact that he had a fashionable apartment in New York City and another in Paris. Of course there was the mansion in Dallas, but as far as she was concerned Dallas was still the frontier. She longed to be back in Paris. Teddy Mack said it wasn't a good idea with a war going on.

She'd been married to a German Count before she found Teddy Mack. It was just as well that he had expired. Had he lived, she'd have been on the wrong side of a war. Unfortunately the Count hadn't left her with a great deal of money. He said once that he spent everything on her. Turns out it was true. All that was left of his estate was a run-down old castle on the Rhine River.

Fortunately, Mr. and Mrs. Theodore Mack Barby were in Paris, where Celeste and the Count had made their home. Celeste met them at an exhibition of impressionist art, organized in part by the famous artist Edgar Degas. Celeste was not particularly interested in Degas or the Impressionists. But the exhibition was being talked about by many of the notables of Paris who were sure to be there. Being in want of a rich husband, now that the Count and his money were gone, she couldn't afford to miss any important social event. Besides, she did love opportunities to be seen and admired.

She struck up an acquaintance with the Barby couple. Mrs. Barby bought paintings by Edgar Degas, Claude Monet, and Pierre-Auguste Renoir. "They are the changing the way we think about art," Mrs. Barby said.

A little discreet checking and Celeste decided it was worth seeing them socially. Lucille Barby was a silly thing with no fashion sense who liked to talk about politics, books, and art. It was a great trial to endure her company. But they became such "good friends" that Celeste was able to be a great source of comfort to Teddy Mack when Lucille fell from the top of the long spiraling staircase at a party and died. The clumsy woman tripped—over Celeste's foot, it so happened. She gave her a little shove to help her along the way, too, though nothing was said about that since Celeste was the only witness. After a slightly less than decent period of mourning, Celeste had Teddy Mack and his money all to herself.

Life would have been perfect except for one thing: the Last Crystal. Her twin brother, C'lestin, would have said that she stole all the crystals—there were seven of them in the beginning. Celeste preferred to think that she chose to put them to better use than he would have. One by one she used the water held inside each to stay young and beautiful until there was only one left. She had been in and out of history, astonishing the ancient Nabataeans in the sandstone city of Petra, Zulu Kings, Pharaohs of Egypt, Roman Emperors, Nordic warriors, and Mayan Kings.

A time would come when she needed the crystal. But there was no reason to trouble herself about it. She had wasted far too much time trying to track it down. If anyone opened the boxes that held it, she would know. If that should happen, she would set her mind to getting it back.

Celeste busied herself with the fine stable of horses Teddy Mack kept. Other than parties, fashion, adventure, and being admired for her breathtaking beauty there wasn't a lot that interested Celeste. But fine horses did interest her. Once, at least a thousand years ago, she was married to a Sheikh who raised fine Arabian horses. She became a skilled judge of horseflesh and a superb rider. She loved horse races, too.

Over the years, she maintained her interest in horses. Now it amused her to appear at The Royal Ascot Races in London on opening day. She enjoyed watching the races. Most of all, she enjoyed being the most beautiful woman there.

Now that she was married to a rich Texas rancher, Celeste wanted to raise a colt herself. She wanted to find one strong enough to win all three of the most important races in the United States: the Kentucky Derby, the Preakness, and the Belmont. She liked to imagine how astoundingly beautiful she would look placing the winner's wreath on her two-year-old champion. Teddy Mack said the best place to find that kind of colt was the great horse show at the Oklahoma State Fair. Many of the horses on display at the show had an impressive lineage.

Teddy Mack said they should arrive at the horse show early before the final round of livestock judging. Never one for early arrivals, Celeste consented only because she wanted the best seats and there was no option to reserve them ahead of the horse show. It was most gratifying, though, to bring the livestock judging to a momentary halt when she entered the stands on Teddy Mack's arm. He was a fine looking man. Besides being wealthy, he made a suitable backdrop for her astounding beauty.

"Looks like this is the bucket calf judgin'," said Teddy Mack.

"Bucket calf?" asked Celeste.

"The little fellers. Usually weaned early. That is as fine a lookin' bunch as I've seen. Look at that white-faced Hereford. He'd be my pick."

Celeste was looking, but not at the calf. The face of the boy leading the white-faced Hereford was exactly like one emblazoned on her mind. It was the face of the girl dressed as a boy who stole the Last Crystal from her. She could remember it vividly, staring at her from the black alabaster box where she had kept it securely for thousands of years. It brought back the jarring realization that without that crystal, she could not go on indefinitely.

Celeste watched the judging in a daze. Thoughts played tag through her mind. That girl had grown up. She and her family died when their house was set on fire. All of them. There was a boy, but nobody escaped that fire. It couldn't be him, could it?

"I never knew you were so interested in cattle," said Teddy Mack, noticing her intense gaze.

"I must talk to that boy," said Celeste.

The judging ended. "The first prize winner will go to the Best of Show competition tomorrow at 11:00 AM," said the judge. Then, after a dramatic pause, he announced, "And the winner is Big Red, a white-faced Hereford shown by his owner, James Matthias from Sage, Oklahoma. Congratulations, James on a fine showing." There was applause as James led Big Red around the arena.

"I do like that calf, Teddy Mack," Celeste said, waving and blowing a kiss to James.

"Told you he was a fine lookin' animal," said Teddy Mack. "Can I pick a winner, or what?"

"I want him," she said.

"Well, I reckon you can make the boy an offer. He'll be here tomorrow."

Celeste was so distracted she was barely able to focus on the horse show that followed. In the end, she let Teddy Mack do the bidding.

"Aren't you feelin' well, Lovely?" asked Teddy Mack as the horse show ended. "Lovely" was his pet name for her. "Not like you to miss out on the bidding. You're better'n me and I can just about out bid anybody if I have a mind to. The trick is to intimidate everybody early so they drop out."

Celeste wasn't paying any attention. "Let's go to the Best of Show judging tomorrow," said Celeste. "I can meet the boy afterward."

"You're still thinkin' about that bucket calf!" said Teddy Mack. "Anyway, I just bought you the finest yearling in the show. You're gonna' love this little fellow."

"I want that calf," she said firmly.

"No reason you can't have them both," he said.

Chapter 13

BEST OF SHOW

Mama and Maggie went home with Hank and Norma Jean Bates. Some of the other contestants left their pens, now that judging was over. But there were a few others there all night along with James and Papa.

The next morning Papa bought coffee, milk and two big cinnamon rolls from a vendor who opened early. James was just finishing the last of his roll when a boy came with a message for him. It was hand written on very fine paper:

Dear James Matthias:

Congratulations on showing a first-rate calf. I am interested in buying him. If you aren't interested in selling, perhaps you can at least afford me the very great pleasure of meeting you and Big Red. I will be attending the Best of

*Show judging at the arena. I will plan to meet
you at the entrance to the arena immediately
following the awards. I will be wearing a blue
hat with red and white flowers. Good luck to
you and Big Red.*

Sincerely,

Mrs. Theodore Mack Barby.

Ordinarily, Celeste refused any name but
Celeste. But, as she wrote the note, it occurred
to her that it might be wise to use her husband's
name.

"I don't want to sell him, Papa," said James
after reading the note aloud.

"You don't have to if you don't want to," said
Papa. "Still, it will be interesting to see what she
would be willing to pay. You can meet her. I'll
be there to support you. Who knows, you might
change your mind."

"Not my Big Red!" said James, smiling up at
Papa. He didn't want to sell, but it was a good
feeling to know other people thought Big Red
was as special as he did.

Papa left to take a seat in the stands with Mama
and Maggie along with Mr. and Mrs. Bates. Mrs.
Bates had won a blue ribbon and first place for
her quilt. It was entered in the women's Best of
Show for handwork that afternoon. It was all
very exciting.

James joined the line of animals that had made it to the final event. There were sheep, horses, cattle, goats, and pigs. As they made their way around the arena in a grand parade, James saw a woman in a big blue hat with red and white flowers. It was the beautiful lady who had caused such a stir yesterday. She was with the man in the white cowboy hat. They waved at him.

James did not win Best of Show. The prize went to a sheep. But he was runner up and won another blue ribbon. At first it was disappointing. But, as he thought about it, James realized that to have made it to the final competition was a great honor. Big Red did his best. So did he. Papa always said, "Give it your best, that is the most anybody can do."

When the judging for Best of Show was over, James and Big Red waited near the entrance to the arena where Papa said they'd meet. He watched the sheep and his owner parade around the arena. "It could have been us, Big Red," he said, patting Big Red on the neck. "It would have been nice to win, but being runner up is nothing to sneeze at." He wondered what the lady in the blue hat would have to say about Big Red.

"So you are James Matthias," said Celeste, hurrying up to greet him. "I'm Mrs. Barby." She'd sent Teddy Mack on an errand so she could have a chance to talk with James alone.

"I'm so sorry," she said in a very sympathetic voice. "Mr. Barby and I were sure that Big Red would win."

"It's okay, Mrs. Barby," said James. "We're really proud that we made it this far."

"As well you should be," said Celeste, sweetly. "Tell me about Sage. I've never been there."

James told her about Main Street, the general store, the post office, the school on the edge of town.

"And do you live in Sage?" she asked when he paused for breath. "I suppose you'd have to live on a farm. I can't imagine raising a calf in town." She smiled sweetly at him. Without giving him a chance to answer, she said, "You so remind me of someone I knew many years ago. Tell me, have you always lived in Sage?"

There was something about the woman's eyes that made James very uncomfortable. He wanted to look away, but it was hard. It was almost as if they commanded him to look. "Don't you want to know about Big Red?" he asked, looking away. It seemed like he knew that voice, if he could just remember.

"I do want to know about Big Red, but I want to know about you, too. The owner of an animal is very important. It makes all the difference." She smiled, her direct gaze unwavering.

James stifled a yawn, avoiding looking directly into her eyes. "Excuse me," he said.

"Now, my dear, tell me all about yourself," she said.

By the time Papa and Mama made their way to where James was waiting, Celeste knew that he was adopted, that he was found on the steps of the church with the map, abalone shell, and Old Shep. "Why you poor dear," she said. "Don't you know anything at all about where you were born?" She wasn't best pleased when Mama and Papa arrived carrying little Maggie. What is more, she was completely dumbfounded when she saw Maggie. James was adopted, but she understood that Maggie was not. Yet, the little girl looked so much like him that it threw her off. Seeing Maggie broke her concentration. More importantly, it broke her hold on James.

Suddenly James felt as if he had been awakened from a dream.

Celeste quickly recovered. "You must be the parents. I am so happy to meet you. James is a remarkable boy!" she said sweetly.

"We think so," said Mama.

"I understand you are interested in buying Big Red, Mrs. Barby," said Papa.

"Why yes, I am interested." Celeste was distracted. James was adopted, but the little girl? Maybe she'd misunderstood. She was too young

116

to be the little girl in that family, the little girl who had opened the box and told her how to find that wretched Grace Willis who stole her crystal from the alabaster box. It was confusing. Celeste could not tolerate confusion.

"He isn't for sale," said James.

"Who?" Celeste asked.

"We can make you a good offer, young man." Teddy Mack Barby arrived. He was a tall, lanky, friendly-looking man. He was only a bit taller than Celeste, who was taller than Mama or Papa. "He'd make a fine addition to our herd."

"Thank you, but he's too much a part of the family," said James. "I'd miss him."

"I can't blame you for wantin' to keep him," said Mr. Barby. "But, think it over. As he gets older, you may change your mind. We could make it worth your while." Mr. Barby gave him a card. "This is how you can reach me. That's a fine calf and you handled him well. We were sure he'd win Best of Show. As far as we're concerned, he is Best of Show!"

Celeste reluctantly said good-bye. Unfortunately there was no way to get James alone now. She felt certain that there must be some connection to the girl who had stolen the crystal and her family. If only she'd had a few more minutes. But at least she knew where James lived. Now she could plan her strategy.

Chapter 14

TALK OF WAR

When they got back to Big Red's pen, all of the side that had been painted brown was covered with yellow letters. "Krauts go home!"

"Oh dear!" said Mama. "Not again. Somebody has seen your name over the stall and recognized it as German. Maybe they're jealous of Big Red's win."

"It's all this war talk and that National Security League," said Papa as he grimly helped James clear Big Red's stall. "They mean well, but they don't have their facts straight. And they don't leave room for difference of opinion. So you get this kind of mischief." They reported the incident to an official and took Big Red home. No more was said about the paint and its ugly message. Papa put the blue ribbon and the certif-icate over Big Red's stall in the barn.

"Now we have a celebrity in the family," said Mama the next day. There was a picture of James and Big Red in the Cedar Hills paper. There was an even bigger picture of Mrs. Bates. She took Best of Show for her quilt. "That's enough excitement for one small town!" said Mama.

When James picked up Patsy on the way to school, Mr. Bates congratulated him. "That's a mighty fine calf, James. You did a good job trainin' him, too. You can have a good animal, but if he isn't well trained he won't show well. We're all proud of you."

"We're proud of Mrs. Bates, too," said James. "To think, she won Best of Show at the State Fair!"

At school, Mr. Tipton announced that Patsy Bates' mother had won Best of Show for her quilt at the State Fair. Then he announced that James won first prize in the calf competition and runner up for Best of Show. Everybody knew. Most of the children had already congratulated him on the playground before school started. But there were some who hung back with Claude, sneering. James stayed away from them.

It wasn't long after they came home from the fair that James got a letter. He read it aloud at the dinner table:

Dear James,

Mr. Barby and I know that you are not inter-ested in selling Big Red. But in the coming weeks, we are going to be visiting Western Oklahoma farms and ranches looking for stock to improve our herd. I hope that we will be able to see you. We shall stop by as we pass through.

Sincerely,

Mrs. Theodore Mack Barby.

"She must have been impressed with Big Red," said Mama.

"Well, I suppose rich folk are used to getting what they want," said Papa. "She may think she'll wear you down, James."

"She can't have Big Red," said James.

Meanwhile there was more talk of war in the papers. There were no incidents in their small community, but German-American families were being harassed in other towns close by.

"I worry about this National Security League," said Mama. They were just sitting down to dinner one evening. She'd been reading the newspaper. "It sounds like they are trying to get the United States to build a bigger army. Anybody who doesn't agree with them is suspect. Now they're talking about asking German-Americans to take loyalty oaths. For goodness sake! This is my country, too. I was born here."

"It's a good way to drum up support for entering the war," said Papa. "It may lead to more of the kind of mischief we saw at the fair, James. People get excited and they don't always think sensibly, even good people like those who live in Sage."

"Some of the kids at school think America should enter the war," said James.

"Most of their parents do, too," said Papa.

"But we don't?" asked James.

"No. War has been around for thousands of years," said Papa. "It hasn't solved problems yet. It just puts them off. It creates hatred and resentment, too. If everybody refused to fight, we couldn't have wars."

"There'll be a time when you have to make up your mind what you believe, James," said Mama. "That is a decision you have to make for yourself. But your Daddy and I believe that God wants us to love, not to hate. It takes far more courage to love than it does to hate."

"You can't be a good soldier and think about the person you're shooting at as another human being," said Papa. "Everybody you point your gun at has a Mama and Papa and maybe even a little sister. They have friends. They have a life they want to live. If we looked across enemy lines and saw every enemy soldier as a person who loves and is loved, how could we kill them?"

Chapter 14

James wasn't sure what he thought about it. More and more of the kids at school talked about the US entering the war and killing all the Krauts. But except for Claude and his friends, nobody called him names.

"What about all those people they're killing? Shouldn't we help them?" he asked Papa one Saturday morning. They had just finished chores and were bringing in the milk.

"Well, Son," said Papa, "I said that I don't believe in fighting. That's not quite true. I don't believe in killing people." He set the pails of milk he was carrying down in the separator room. "But there are other ways to fight. Sometimes you have to be willing to take a stand, maybe even risk being killed."

"I don't know what I'd do if somebody came after you or Maggie," said Mama, holding the door to the kitchen open for them. "I hope I wouldn't kill anybody. I hope I'd have the courage to try and save you another way."

"Human life is so valuable, Son," said Papa. "Opposing violence is a hard way to live. I don't know if I could watch somebody being harmed and not step in and fight. I'd like to think that I'd put myself between those fighting and stop the violence. But it's the idea that I live toward. Thank God I've never been put to that test. I honestly believe that when you meet violence with violence, nobody wins."

Little Maggie, who had already begun her breakfast, brought the conversation to a halt by putting her bowl of oatmeal on her head. As the oatmeal began dripping down she had a surprised look on her face, then burst into tears. "Quick, James! Get me a wet washcloth," said Mama. "You didn't expect that, did you Maggie?"

When he handed her the washcloth, Mama said, "I'd like you to collect some black walnuts. They should be ready now. Once you get that done, you can have the day to yourself unless Papa needs you." She began wiping oatmeal from a squirming Maggie. "There, there. That will hold you."

Maggie clapped her hands and began calling, "Down, Maggie wants down."

"If there are any left on the trees and you can reach them, get those. If not pick up any with green husks that you can find on the ground," said Mama. She gave him the same directions every year. James knew exactly what to do without being told. "Don't forget your gloves," she added. "You don't want black walnut stain all over your hands." He knew that too.

"I have to run in to the hardware store," said Papa. "Maybe when I get back we can see about getting the husks off of the walnuts." It was a job James hated.

Taking a couple of buckets, James headed across the pasture to the black walnut grove that bordered one edge of their property. The buckets were nearly full when he happened to notice an odd bit of green in a gnarled place on one of the older trees. It wasn't a walnut. It was too big and it wasn't quite that shade of green. Looking more closely, James caught his breath. A Luna Moth, wings spread wide, was held there as if it had been carefully mounted. He could tell that it was dead. It didn't move when he gently touched it. How long it had been dead, he couldn't say. James had never seen a Luna Moth or been lucky enough to find a dead one. He gently removed it from the tree. It was a big moth and in perfect condition. The spreading wings were almost five inches across. Its white body and pinkish legs were petrified. He looked at the antenna. A male Luna Moth has lots of hairs on the antenna, he reminded himself. This moth had narrower antenna with less hair than he'd expect a male to have. It must be a female, he thought. They like to lay eggs on the back of black walnut leaves. The big eyespots along the back wings and long tails were in perfect condition. Finding it more than made up for having to pick up black walnuts. He couldn't wait to get back to the house and show Mama. She wasn't enthusiastic about moths, but she'd share his excitement.

When he got back, there was a big, red touring car sitting in the driveway. The few cars around Sage were not so grand as this one. James guessed right away that it belonged to Mr. and Mrs. Barby. He set the buckets on the back porch, took off his gloves, and went in, carrying the moth.

Chapter 15

THE H & R SWATHE
SECURITY COMPANY

"That Grace Willis warn't all bad," said Junior. He stretched as the first light of morning hit the old Swathmore dugout. "We used to have some good times when we was all here."

"I think our Ma and Pa was meaner to her than they was to us. And that's sayin' somethin'. Maybe that's why she run off," said Ruby. There was something akin to sadness in her voice. "Lets get some grub and get out of here."

As they ate a can of cold beans each, Ruby spotted something. "Lookie there, Junior. Reckon what's in that box?" A wooden crate lay on its side in one corner.

Junior turned it over, disgusted with what he found. "Just books. Must have left 'em when we moved over to the Tradin' Post. What was we doin' with a bunch 'a books?"

"Hmm," said Ruby, picking them up. "These was Grace's books I reckon. Ma kept 'em hid from her. Grace thought they was, *were*,"— Ruby corrected herself, suddenly remembering her resolution to improve—"Grace thought they were left behind on the Santa Fe Trail. I heard Ma tellin' Pa oncet after Grace run off. Wasn't much of a mother, was she? Downright mean. Bone lazy, too. Can't think why she had it in for Grace." She poked around in the box. "Lookie, Junior. This here is *Aladdin and His Wonderful Lamp.* She used to tell us this story. See the lamp on the cover? Reckon I'll take it."

"Got me an idea," said Junior, opening one of the books. The book was in good condition, despite years in the dugout. He took his knife and cut a large section out of the middle. "That'll hold 'em."

Soon they had the few books that had belonged to Grace cut out with notes stuffed in them—all except the Aladdin book and one other that Ruby wouldn't let Junior have.

"What cha want that 'en fer?" asked Junior, eyeing the book Ruby hugged to her chest. "It ain't even got pictures. It's a big 'en, too. We could stash the rest of the notes in it."

"This here is one of them books as has got all the words in the world in it," said Ruby. "Figure I might learn some of 'em."

"Can't think why," said Junior, disgruntled.

"I wish she hadn't said what she did before I shot her," said Ruby, thumbing through the dictionary.

"What'd she say? I didn't hear nothin'," said Junior.

"Looked me in the eye. Didn't even look scared. Didn't whimper or cry or nothin'. Just said, 'Ruby, don't do it. You're better'n this.' I was pullin' on the trigger and she said it all calm like she was askin' the time of day, 'Please Ruby, at least spare the chil'ren.'" There was a catch in Ruby's voice. "She had it wrong. I weren't better. We killed 'em all. She was the only one who ever had a word of kindness fer us, except fer her mamma. And I went and shot her."

"Quit frettin' over it, Ruby. Like I said, we was employed. You was doin' your job."

"I don't want a job like that anymore," said Ruby. She picked up the piles of scrap paper that Junior had left on the floor and put them on the fire. They made a bright blaze.

"Best be haulin' ourselves outta here," said Junior, putting the last of the books in his bulging saddlebags. The gold coin was distributed between pockets and saddlebags.

Chapter 15

Ruby left Junior to get the packhorses loaded while she filled their canteens at the creek spring. She was caught up watching how the spring bubbled over, remembering days long gone when a sound that was out of place jerked her back into the present. She wasn't sure, it might have been the snap of a twig. Instantly dropping to the ground, she flattened herself behind the low brush that grew along the creek bank. She heard voices before she could see what was happening.

"Drop the bag. Hands up high where as we can see 'em," said a strong, male voice.

Ruby caught her breath. Dropping the saddlebag he'd been holding, Junior slowly raised his hands. He was looking up the barrel of Grat Dalton's rifle. Backing up Grat were Dick Bradwell and Bill Powers. Emmett and Bob Dalton were nowhere to be seen. Ruby felt pretty sure they were close by, probably looking for her.

"Reckon you have somethin' that belongs to us," said Grat.

Junior was calm under pressure. "Yeah, reckon so. Can't blame a fella for stealin' somethin' ta eat. Reserves was getting' low. Guess I figured y'all wouldn't miss a bit of cornmeal."

Bill Powers grinned, holding up the cornmeal sack Junior emptied when they redistributed the money. "Yeah? I'd say this one held some mighty fine cornmeal." He reached in and pulled out a single gold coin, holding it up to the light.

Ruby began stealthily inching her way around to the back of the dugout. She wanted to know exactly where Emmett and Bob were before she made her move.

Junior kept his head. She knew he would. Nobody could do it better. "I told you I was gettin' low on grub. But if you need it worse 'n I do, hep yourself. Heck, I didn't even touch y'all's whiskey. Been dryer'n an old bone, too."

When she was out of view, Ruby stood in a crouched position, guns out. She crept around the far side of the dugout. Bob Dalton, gun drawn, stood near the entrance to the dugout looking around while his brother, Emmett, shook one of the bedrolls just outside the dugout door. They'd left a mess. Everything that wasn't in the saddle-bags had been gone through and dumped. The suit that Celeste and the Count had bought for Junior lay on the ground along with blankets from his bedroll. Emmett let the one dress and bonnet she had rolled up in her bedroll drop to the ground. "Told you one of 'em was a woman. That'll make it easier," he grinned. "Reckon where she got off to?"

"Hope she's prettier'n that son-of-a-gun," grinned Bob, nodding toward Junior.

"Drop the gun, Bob. Both of you, hands up or you're dead," she ordered in a low voice, standing tall. "Not a word outta ya." They were in full view of Junior and the rest of the gang who were occupied with taking the contents out of his saddlebags. She was pretty sure Junior saw her; he didn't look her way. He knew better.

Bob dropped his gun. Both men put their hands up. Keeping her voice low and calm, she said, "Now you gonna take one hand and slowly unbuckle that gun belt, Emmett. Keep the other'n up. We gonna keep this real quiet like. One false move and you an' Bob's both dead." She watched as Emmett began to slowly reach for his gun belt. "My trigger finger is mighty touchy, Emmett. Don't neither one of you boys make me nervous. Keep both hands high up where as I can see 'em, Bob."

Bob stood grinning at her, hands high, "Yep, Emmett. She is prettier." Ruby ignored the comment. Emmett had his gun belt unbuckled now.

"Toss that gun belt my way, Emmett, nice and easy. I wanna see one hand high," Ruby ordered quietly.

Suddenly Emmett hurled the gun belt at her. At the same instant Bob took a dive for his gun.

With split second timing, she dodged the gun belt and shot Bob's gun before he could hit the ground, narrowly missing his hand. Her other shot scattered the dirt at Emmett's feet. He jumped out of the way.

Simultaneously, Bill Powers and Dick Bradwell whirled around, guns aimed at Ruby. But she had maneuvered herself so that Emmett stood in the way, making it tricky for either of them to get a good, clear shot at her.

"Bob, you better ask Grat which one of you he wants to die first," she said loudly, all casual like. She pointed one gun at his head and the other at Emmett's. "Yer buddies over there are lookin' at me in a real unfriendly way."

Bob started to push himself up off the ground. "You can stay down there seein' as that's where you wanted to be," said Ruby grimly. "The only reason you still have that right hand Bob, is 'cause I wasn't aimin' at it. Don't make me shoot it off. I'd hate you to lose your means of livelihood."

Bob wasn't grinning anymore.

Everything came to a standstill for a few seconds. Grat's rifle was aimed at Junior. Junior held his hands high the air. Bill and Dick had guns aimed at Ruby. Ruby's pistols were pointed at Emmett and Bob.

"Reckon we can work this out," said Bob, still flat on the ground.

"Yep. Reckon we can," said Ruby in a calm, reasonable voice. She kept her eye on all five of them.

Bob began to push himself up, the grin returning to his face.

"Stay where you are, Bob. You can put those hands behind your head, too," warned Ruby in a deceptively friendly voice. "I think I see what you're getting' at. You sweet-talk me whilst Grat shoots Junior. Emmett falls to the ground so as Dick and Bill can get a strait shot at me. Except, any of that happens and you're dead. I'll shoot you and Emmett before they can drop me." She could tell they were sizing her up, trying to decide if they could get away with it.

"Don't none of that sound very pretty to me," said Ruby, watching the grin leave Bob's face altogether. "Seems like a lot of blood over one bag of cornmeal. And it warn't even full. I got me a better plan. Drop the rifle, Grat. Put your hands up high and out where as I can see 'em, slow and easy, away from those pistols. Same for you two, Dick and Bill, drop your guns nice and easy like, lessen you want me to shoot these two. I don't have a mind to kill anybody, but you decide. One unfortunate move and they's both dead."

Grat dropped the rifle. Taking his lead, Dick and Bill dropped theirs, slowly spreading out their hands and raising them above their heads. Junior picked up the rifle. "Good choice, Grat," he said. "I ain't ever knowed anybody as could outshoot Ruby. Now I want to see that gun belt drop to the ground, slowly. Keep one hand in the air. Wouldn't do to make Ruby nervous. She might shoot Bob and Emmett." Grat unbuckled his gun belt slowly and let it drop.

Junior marched Grat over to where Dick and Bill stood, kicking their guns out of reach, making them drop their gun belts. "Now down on your belly, boys, hands behind your head so as I can keep y'all out of trouble." One by one he made the three men get up, tying each to a tree in his turn. Ruby had Bob back on his feet. Both he and Emmett were backed up to trees by the time Junior was ready for them.

When the last of the gang was tied fast, Junior picked up their guns. "We ain't gonna keep yer guns, fellas. But I'm a puttin' 'em outta reach. You can keep yer horses, too. There's an old abandoned homestead jest up this side 'a the creek thata way." He nodded toward the Cimarron River. "Oncet y'all's figured out how to free yerselves it won't take more'n a couple 'a hours to get there on foot. Grat, I'm leavin' your gun belt here." He hurled it as far as he could throw it away from them. "You might need one set of guns on ya. I'll thank y'all to make it the last time we ever sets eyes on each other. We's doin' this out of respect for y'all's work. But I won't show no mercy next time."

Ruby got the canteens she'd left by the creek. They calmly finished packing up. As they started to lead the horses away, she turned back. "Reckon y'all's found the big cavern where we was holed up. Made a mighty fine home for us. Ain't a lawman been able to find it yet. Y'all wouldna found it neither if it warn't for that gall durn hole in the meal sack. I'm callin' it even. You keep what you got, we keeps what we got. Don't mess with us again." With that she turned and led her horses away.

They found the horses left by the Dalton gang around a bend in the creek, still saddled. They'd been sitting ducks for the Daltons. "Junior, it was fools luck that had me at the creek when they crept up on us. One more reason we should ought to find another line of work."

"Yeah, but we bested 'em, didn't we?" said Junior, grinning all over. "Ain't anybody I know of as can say that."

"Reckon we ought to leave their horses here?" asked Ruby.

"Well, our horses is warmed up now, let's high tail it outta here. It'll take 'em a few minutes to get free. They'll get over here 'bout as fast as we did walkin' our horses. Tell you what, we'll give the horses their freedom. They won't go far. By the time they round 'em up, we'll be long gone. They'll go for their guns before they tries to track us."

"Best take the saddles off, then," said Ruby. "Won't take a minute and that'll slow 'em down more."

It was just shy of an hour's ride at a gallop to the old homestead and it had them backtracking. It seemed only fair, though, since they were making off with the money they'd taken from the Dalton's stash. They'd never made a practice of stealing from other thieves. They hung the gun belts on a broken down split rail fence. Junior propped Grat's rifle up against the fence. "Bein' kinder than we should oughta be," said Ruby.

"Well, the way I sees it, Grat coulda shot before he asked questions," said Junior, turning his horse. "He was showin' respect."

"They wasn't showin' me no respect," said Ruby.

"They was by the time you was through with 'em," Junior grinned.

"I don't call that respect," said Ruby. "Anyways, we ain't givin' 'em another opportunity."

"Reckon if we cut through headed at an angle, we ought to hit that old trail to the Tradin' Post without back-trackin'," said Junior, eyeing the horizon. "They'll be on our tail in an hour or so, the way I reckon it. Too much money to let it go."

"That's what I'm thinkin'," said Ruby.

They worked their horses as hard as they dared on the unbroken prairie. They found the trail to the Trading Post overgrown, but much easier going. They didn't try to cover their tracks. Speed and distance were what counted. They rode late and started early, well before dawn, camping with no fire and one of them on watch. When they got as far as the Trading Post, they could see that it had changed hands since their Pa's days. There was a whole town built up around it now. They didn't ask any questions. They sold their horses for half of what they were worth, bought a trunk, and left on the next stagecoach to Amarillo, Texas.

A few days later, a very respectable couple with a large trunk caught the train in Amarillo, headed for San Francisco on the St. Louis to San Francisco railroad line. They'd both had a bath. Ruby wore the dress Celeste had given her and Junior was dressed in his suit and clean-shaven. Nobody recognized them. Once in San Francisco, they dropped more from Swathmore, added an e and gave it a fancy pronunciation. It was Ruby's idea, "Swath sounds like cuttin' hay. 'Sway-the' sounds more cultured-like."

"Huh?" said Junior. He found everything about starting over puzzling.

"You can't be Junior, neither. From now on, you goina be Hiram." In San Francisco they melted into the great crowds of people who had flocked there during the gold rush to make their fortune and stayed on.

Hiram Swathe and his sister Ruby eventually made their way to Sacramento. With Ruby's prodding they set up the H & R Swathe and Company of Sacramento, training and providing a team of highly skilled professional guards to protect banks, businesses, and trains. Ruby ran the company. She got Hiram to read by pointing out that if he couldn't read the work orders, particularly when payrolls were being transferred from banks to company headquarters, people could pull all kinds of shenanigans. It wasn't enough to just read the numbers. When he found a purpose in it, even Hiram could learn to read.

Ruby begin a side business of her own: R. Swathe Protection Training for the Discrete and Discerning Woman. It was for women who wanted to learn how to carry and use a gun without everybody knowing it. Women from some of Sacramento's finest families privately flocked to her. She taught them how to shoot and taught them they didn't have to take disrespect from anybody—with or without a gun to protect them.

Junior was happy as a toad in a puddle. But Ruby was haunted by nightmares.

Chapter 16

THE LUNA MOTH

Mr. and Mrs. Barby sat in the parlor with Mama and Maggie. In her playpen, Maggie wanted out. She was getting big for a playpen, but ordinarily, she loved being there with her toys. Now she held on the sides, jumping up and down. When she saw James, she began calling, "Ames! Ames! Maggie wants out."

"Here's our boy!" exclaimed Celeste. She stood up all smiles.

"Hello there, young man," said Mr. Barby. He stood, too. "Changed your mind about Big Red?" He heartily shook James' hand.

"No sir," said James.

"Didn't think so, but when your daddy gets back I'd like to have a look at his herd. Big Red comes from good stock," said Mr. Barby.

"What is that you have?" asked Celeste, looking at the moth James was holding in one hand. She was feeling very satisfied. Before James returned she remarked about how much Maggie looked like him. She got Hannalore to talking about how James had been adopted and how Maggie wasn't. Hannalore even told her that James had helped name Maggie. There had been a little sister, Grace. It was one of the few things he remembered of his past. With the right prompting, Celeste felt sure James might remember more. Best of all, Grace was the name of the little sister who had opened the wooden box, looked into her eyes, and talked with her years ago. It was how she was able to track down Grace Willis. The girl seemed to be out of the way now. How James managed to escape the fire that took the rest of his family, she'd probably never know. But she knew enough. If he had the crystal, it wouldn't take her long to find out.

"Why that's a Luna Moth, Lovely. A fine specimen, James," said Mr. Barby, having a look at it. "Female. It's late in the year for them."

"That's what I thought," said James. "I figured maybe it settled there in that protected place before it died."

"You hardly ever see one of these," Mr. Barby explained to Celeste. "They only fly at night.

Don't live more than about a week. I reckon that if you wanted to find one as fine as this, you'd have to camp out under a black walnut tree all summer."

"James has a moth collection," said Mama.

"How interesting!" exclaimed Celeste. "Maybe you could show us."

Mama laughed. "You are braver than I am. I'm happy for James to have his collection. But there is something about all those impaled moths that gives me the shivers. If you'd like to show them, James, why don't you take your boxes out to the table on the back porch."

Just then, Papa returned. There were more greetings. Mama said she'd make coffee while they all went out to see Big Red and look over the herd.

Celeste had other plans. "Oh, but James, would you mind awfully showing me your collection first? Maybe we could join the others afterward. That way I can say, 'Hello,' to Big Red. Mr. Barby is the real judge of cattle. I do so want to see all your moths."

James agreed, hurrying to bring the stack of wooden cigar boxes holding his collection. Celeste held the door to the back porch for him. She was all smiles.

"I have moth balls in all these boxes," he warned. "That keeps the moths safe from other pests."

"How very clever," she said. "Why did you decide to collect moths instead of butterflies?"

"It started at school," he explained. "We found one in the classroom room and I thought it was pretty. Miss More—she was my teacher—showed me how to mount it. It was this one, the Red-tailed Specter." James opened the first of his boxes, pointing to a white moth with black markings across the upper wings and red on the body. There were several moths in the box.

Celeste asked about each one. They went through all the boxes. "You say this is a Harnessed Tiger Moth?" She pointed to the last one, "It's wings look almost like stained glass. Isn't that remarkable?" She spoke softly and gently. "Tell me, James, if you could have any moth in the world that you don't have, what would it be?"

James didn't hesitate. "It would be the Polyphemus Moth."

"Tell me about that moth," she said, looking in his eyes.

It made James uncomfortable. He looked away. "Well the Polyphemus is one of the silk moths. They're the largest moths. The Luna Moth I just found is a silk moth. They are in this part of Oklahoma, but I've never found one. The

Polyphemus is named for Polyphemus in Greek mythology."

"Oh yes, I remember him. The giant Cyclops— one eye in the middle of his forehead. Ugly fellow," said Celeste, shivering. "You wouldn't want to meet him. No personality, either." She almost forgot herself lost in her memory for a moment.

"Yes, it gets the name because of the large eyespots in the middle of its hind wings. It's tan colored," said James.

"I would love to get you that moth," said Celeste, looking directly into his eyes again. "And there is another. I know you would like it. It is the Madagascan Sunset Moth. It flies in the daytime. I'm not sure, it may be one of the only moths that does that. I'm not expert, you see," she smiled sweetly "It comes from Madagascar, a huge island off the coast of Africa. Its name comes from its beautiful colors, like the sunset: turquoise, red, orange. It is such a beautiful moth. Some people think it is the most valuable moth in the whole world. I want you to have it." Her voice was like a soft running stream.

She looked steadily at James smiling, speaking slowly, softly. "You look puzzled, James. Do you know why I want to do this for you?" Without giving him a chance to answer, she said, in the same, soft voice, "Look at me. This is important. I want to do this because I knew your mother, not Mrs. Mathias, but your real mother. She was about your age when I first saw her. You look very much like her."

Something wasn't right. James had the uncomfortable feeling that he'd felt before when she talked to him at the fair. He was a bit offended that she spoke as if Mama weren't real. But he wanted to be polite. He would like to have the moths, too. Most of all, he wanted to know more about his birth mother.

"Look at me James," she said softly. "This is very important. Your dear mother had something that belonged to me, but she died before she could return it or tell me where to find it. I wonder, do you know what she had?"

James' mind went back to the memory he first had when Maggie tried to climb up the pen to Claude's calf at the county fair. He remembered Gracie, climbing the ladder, talking with someone who spoke in a soft, sweet voice, a voice like this voice.

"Are you listening James? You aren't looking at me." Celeste's voice was soothing. It made him want to go to sleep.

"Yes ma'm," said James. But he didn't look into her eyes. The ladder, that voice, somebody screaming, No Gracie! Somebody calling for Mr. Nichols. Mr. Nichols! He wanted to call for Mr. Nichols, but he couldn't. He tried to say it out loud, Help, Mr. Nichols, but the words died on his tongue.

"You know where it is, don't you? The thing your mother was keeping for me," Celeste asked gently. "If you do, you must get it for me. I want it back so very much." She spoke steadily, soothingly, like a sigh on the wind. "It would mean even more to me because she kept it for me. I want to do good things for you, James, like getting you the Polyphemus Moth and the Madagascan Sunset Moth. It would be so easy for me to do that. I would so love to."

James thought of the carpetbag on the top shelf in his closet. He wanted to tell her all about it and to go get it for her. But there was something else, something he promised. He covered his mouth as he yawned again. He was so tired and confused, he couldn't think what it was. It was about the carpetbag. "I have a map," he said thickly, looking at Celeste. It was hard to talk.

"A map?" she asked, raising her eyebrows ever so slightly.

"My mother made it for me," he said. Every word was an effort.

"No, dear, not a map."

Something about the way she looked at him made James feel like he was one of the moths stuck through with a pin, unable to move, unable to fly away. "My mother gave me a map." He said again. He wanted to say that somebody gave him a carpetbag, but now he couldn't remember who. And somebody gave him an abalone shell. But he didn't know who that was either. He didn't want to look at her any more. He didn't want the moths.

"Look at me, James," she said sweetly. "It is a beautiful wooden box. You mustn't open the box. But if you know where it is, you can get it for me." She waited a moment, still holding him with her eyes. He felt trapped. He couldn't move.

"A red abalone shell," he mumbled.

"No James. It was a box." She continued, slowly, softly, "If you can't get it right now, you can give it to the men who come to pick up the cattle that Mr. Barby is buying from your Daddy. They will take care of it for me. If you can't get it, you can send me a post card and tell me where to find it. As soon as I have the box your mother kept for me, I will send you the Polyphemus Moth and the Madagascan Sunset Moth. I so want you to have them. But I can't send them until I have the box. I'm afraid that once you have the moths you will forget all about me and how much your dear mother meant to me. I know she would want you to do this."

James wanted her to stop looking at him. He wanted her to stop talking. The carpetbag was on the top shelf of the closet, behind where he kept the moths. He was just about to get up and go get it, even though he didn't want to, when Mr. Barby came striding up the porch steps and opened the screen door.

"Look at you two, thick as thieves," he said. "Let's see that moth collection, James."

Papa was right behind him. He gave James a pat on the back. "You look sleepy, Son. Were you up late last night reading?"

The pat on the back felt like a lifeline to James. Suddenly he was himself again. It was like he'd been fast asleep.

Celeste smiled. She wasn't angry. After all, she had looked into the boy's eyes and told him what he must do. It had never failed. She was almost certain now that despite what she had been told, C'lestin, her interfering twin, had managed to save this boy when the rest of the family was killed. If he knew anything about the crystal, the boy would tell her sooner or later. She was almost sure he knew something.

Mamma called them in for coffee. Afterward, while Papa and Mr. Barby worked out the details for pick-up of the three yearlings Mr. Barby was buying, Celeste said, "James, don't forget what you have to do for me. And I won't forget those two moths. You can always send me a post card. In fact, I have one in my purse. I'll address it for you. There's already a stamp on it."

She handed it to him as they were getting into the big red touring car. "Wouldn't it be nice if we got James a Madagascan Sunset Moth, darling? I want to do something special for him."

146

"Well, Lovely, I don't know anything about that one, but if you want to do that, go right ahead," said Mr. Barby. "I tell you what, Karl. Once Celeste gets something in her pretty little head, there's no turning back." With that he started the car and they were away.

James stood back from the car, looking at the one cent green stamp with the picture of George Washington on it, glad he wasn't looking at Mrs. Barby. When Mr. Barby said, "Celeste," it was like somebody had just pulled the floor right out from under him and he was standing above a bottomless pit, about to fall. He'd almost given her the crystal. "I'm so sorry, Mr. Nichols," he said under his breath. "I'm so sorry." He knew that he hadn't heard the last from Celeste. And he was terribly afraid that he had made a dreadful mistake in agreeing to take care of the crystal. He was making a bad job of it. Worst of all, he feared that the crystal was putting his family in danger. Behind all Celeste's sweet smiles was a truly dreadful person.

"My goodness," said Mama, "I daresay it won't be long before we have a string of people dropping in to see who they were!"

"They were noticeable, that's for sure," laughed Papa. "You're awfully quiet, James. Is something the matter?"

"I don't know," said James honestly. "Mrs. Barby gives me the heebie jeebies."

"She is awfully intense," said Mama. "You probably felt a bit bowled over."

"That's for sure," said James. He wished he could tell them. What would Celeste do if she knew the Last Crystal was sitting on the top shelf of his closet behind the wooden cigar boxes full of moths?"

Chapter 17

A GIRL NAMED CHAWNAWAY

Mama liked to make Sunday Dinner something special. She put out the best dishes and laid out the white linen tablecloth before they left for church. James had to set the table when they got home. But he didn't mind. There was always something wonderful to eat. Sometimes they invited the preacher and his wife over for dinner. Or they had Mr. Tipton and his wife and three children, or Miss Hurley, the new teacher. Nobody was coming for dinner today. James was just as glad. It meant he would have the afternoon to himself. He still felt the shakes after yesterday's visit from the Barbys.

When they finally sat down at the table Mama said, "I told you everybody at church would be asking about who came to see us in that big, fancy red car. I didn't think I'd ever get away."

Chapter 17

"They were curious all right," said Papa. "But it shouldn't have been too surprising to anybody. When you have a big winner at the State Fare, it attracts buyers."

"Norma Jean said that she'd had several letters from people wanting to buy her quilt or for her to make one for them," said Mama. "But nobody else had a big red touring car sitting in their yard. I think Mrs. Barby attracted a lot of attention when they went through town, too, with the top down on the car."

"I have a feeling that is exactly what Mrs. Barby would want," said Papa dryly.

James barely listened to the conversation, preoccupied with his own worries. He'd hardly slept that night and he'd fallen asleep twice during the sermon at church. After dinner he set out for the creek with Old Shep. He had almost broken his promise to Mr. Nichols. He was angry and disappointed in himself. How could he do that for a couple of moths? He wasn't so sure that Celeste really knew his mother, either. She was just trying to trick him into giving her the crystal. But he fell for it. That was the worst of it. He fell for her trick.

He wished Miss More were still here. He really needed to talk to somebody and he didn't want to worry Mama and Papa. He was pretty sure that Celeste would not leave it alone. Though Miss More and her brother and Mr. Nichols hadn't actually said so, he was also pretty sure that she was responsible for his parents being dead. It was a terrible thought. He had to do something to protect Mama, Papa and Maggie. The thought of losing them was unbearable.

He threw a stick for Old Shep to catch. There was a sharp chill in the air that hinted of November. The days were getting shorter. When they got as far as the swimming hole, James thought about the day Claude and his gang tried to jump him. "I wish you were here now, Mr. Nichols," he said aloud. "I'd give you back the crystal."

Old Shep brought back the stick. James threw it again. This time, Old Shep over-ran the stick and kept on going, barking happily. He disappeared into the trees that lined the creek. Something had him excited. It wasn't a rabbit, either. It had to be something bigger. James wondered if it were a deer.

James followed. He saw Song of the Wind before he saw Mr. Nichols.

"Hello, James." Mr. Nichols was sitting on a big rock. "I was expecting you."

James spilled out the whole story. "Don't be so hard on yourself, James. The important thing isn't what you did, it's what you didn't do. Celeste was doing her best to get you in her power. It's true that she had to give up her magical powers when she became a mortal. But she still has powers bound to the crystal. She is very good at manipulating people and getting them to do what she wants. She can be very persuasive when she hypnotizes somebody, too. But the thing is, even if you are hypnotized, it doesn't mean you lose control over your mind or your good judgment. Maybe you were about to get the carpetbag for her, but you didn't. You didn't even tell her about it. You are made of strong stuff, Son."

"But I was on my way to get the carpetbag. If Mr. Barby and Papa hadn't come, I'd have given it to her!"

"I don't think so. About the time you got to your closet, something would have clicked. You'd probably have given her the abalone shell or one of the rocks from your collection. Your mind was resisting her all the time."

James let out a sigh of relief. "She said she knew my mother from before. I didn't even suspect she was Celeste."

"Of course you didn't. She was trying to deceive you. She never knew your mother. She saw her through the alabaster box, when your mother opened it. Your mother was disguised as a boy. For years, she didn't know any different. She saw your little sister Gracie, when she opened the carpetbag and the wooden box. She never even saw you."

"I think I made a mistake when I agreed to look after the crystal," said James. "I don't want to do it anymore."

"Your mother felt that way sometimes, too," said Mr. Nichols. He stood. "I've been studying the matter for some time. I think we'd better put the crystal completely out of her reach. I know now that we can without harming anybody if we do it carefully. You'll have to help. It is too big a responsibility for you to have to keep it here now that I've found another way.

"Would you like to go for a ride? You'll have to get the crystal. And you'll need to bring the map your mother made for you."

"As long as I'm home in time for chores," said James.

"We can do that," said Mr. Nichols, smiling at him. "We've done it before. Old Shep, do you want to come along?"

It wasn't as if Old Shep actually said, "Yes, please. I would like to go." But everything about him said exactly that.

Song of the Wind was never ridden with a saddle. But this time, Mr. Nichols had saddlebags thrown over him. He put the canvas bag he always carried in one of the saddlebags and had James put the carpetbag and map in the other. Song of the Wind broke into a trot, then a full gallop, going so fast James had to shut his eyes and lean into Mr. Nichols. When he began to slow down, James realized they'd been flying. Below he saw the top of a mountain range covered with tall pine trees. Foothills dropped into a wide meadowland on the other side. Beyond that the land stretched out all the way to the sea. It seemed familiar, like something he'd seen in one of the geography books at school. Or had he dreamed it? Or was he remembering again?

Song of the Wind set down below the foot-hills in the meadowland. Low trees followed a creek as it made its way westward toward the sea. In the distance they could see a collection of houses with cone-shaped roofs. They looked like enormous beehives. "We'll have to leave the carpetbag and map with Song of the Wind," Mr. Nichols said, giving Song of the Wind a gentle pat. "I'll call you when I need you." Song of the Wind shook his head as if he understood per-fectly, then disappeared into the tall grass." Old Shep, you come with us," said Mr. Nichols.

James had forgotten Old Shep in the excite-ment of the ride. But there he was, standing where Song of the Wind had set them down, wagging his tail and smiling his doggy smile. James was a bit puzzled, then he remembered what Mr. Nichols once said, Miss More, too. "Old Shep is no ordinary dog."

"We're going to that village up ahead. There's someone I think you'd very much like to see," said Mr. Nichols.

"Gracie?" James was hardly able to believe it. Now he remembered. He had been here before, a long time ago, with Mr. Nichols, on Song of the Wind. Old Shep hadn't come then.

Mr. Nichols nodded. "Yes, but you must not call her Gracie except when you are alone. Her people believe that personal names are to be used very carefully and quietly. She has another name now, Chawnaway."

"She'll be about nine-years-old by now," said James.

"Time is different here, James. You never know how much time has lapsed when you return. It might be a year or it might be fifteen," said Mr. Nichols. "I think you'll find her much older than you expect."

"Will she know me?" James wondered.

Mr. Nichols looked at him and smiled. "What do you think?"

They came upon a group of children playing just outside the village. The children squealed with excitement, jumped up, and ran into the circle of houses, calling. James didn't see Gracie among them. By the time they reached the circle, there was a small collection of men waiting for them. Women stood in the background, looking. Young children peeped out from behind the women. Older children stopped where they were and stared. James searched their faces for Gracie.

The people looked like pictures from one of his schoolbooks. The men were bare from the waist up. They wore a kind of apron skirt that hung from a belt at the waist. Their long hair was pulled back and tied. Women had on apron skirts, too. The younger children weren't bothered about clothes. It looked just as it looked the night Mr. Nichols rescued them.

A man wearing a feathered hat stepped forward, smiling as he greeted Mr. Nichols. James couldn't understand their language, but Mr. Nichols talked with them freely. The man in the cap waved at one of the women, saying something to her.

She hurried away, returning with two tightly woven baskets about the size of a large cup. The baskets were full of hot soup.

As he was finishing his soup, James noticed an old woman with long white hair making her way from one of the houses. She was leaning on the arm of a young girl who was dressed like the others, but something about her was unmistakably different. "Gra…, my sister?" Stopping himself from saying her name, James looked at Mr. Nichols.

Mr. Nichols nodded. "She is a couple of years ahead of you."

James started to run, but suddenly shyness overcame him. His younger sister was now older than he was. The old woman said something to the girl, who left her to come running to James as fast as she could. She threw her arms around him in a big hug. "My very own brother! I've outgrown you." Her English was a little rusty, but he understood her well enough. "And Old Shep!

You've brought Old Shep along." She fell to her knees and threw her arms around Old Shep, who was wagging all over in delight.

The old woman caught up. Leaning over, she gave Old Shep a pat. She said something that James didn't understand except for "Old Shep."

"She's glad to see him again, too," said Gracie. Giving Old Shep a final hug, she returned to her feet.

"Again?" asked James. Old Shep hadn't come with them the first time James was there. He looked at the dog critically, "What is this, the secret life of Old Shep?" Nobody answered him. The old woman was talking rapidly to Gracie and Mr. Nichols.

The old woman turned out to be the village shaman who had promised to rear Gracie as her own daughter. She gave James a new name, Chukauyon'. It meant small, because James was just a bit smaller than his sister Chawnaway now.

They stayed there for more than a month. Chukauyon, shed his clothes to dress like the rest of the men and boys. Every day was full and interesting. One day they went to the ocean with the men in a carved-out canoe made from one log. Old Shep went along, sitting in the canoe as if he'd done it every day of his life. James played with the boys his age. But most of all, he stayed with Gracie and the old woman, who was called Kipo'mo.

James remembered, now. Kipo'mo was the one who gave him the red abalone shell. Gracie told him Kipo'mo was teaching her about plants and herbs for healing. She told him all about life in the village. He told her all about life with the Matthias family.

Once when they were alone, James asked Mr. Nichols, "Can't she come home with me? I know Mama and Papa would welcome her. Maggie would love to have a big sister."

"She is very happy here, James," said Mr. Nichols. "She would never be safe from Celeste if she returned."

"But you said that Celeste couldn't have mind control of anybody just by hypnotizing them. Why isn't she safe?"

"The crystal will stay here, too," Mr. Nichols continued. "But you and I will need to put it somewhere safe, not with Gracie. She is no longer a child, but she has never been safe with it since she fell into Celeste's power. Neither are you, now. We can't trust that you will be safe with the crystal in your care. That isn't hypnosis, that is the dark magic Celeste wrapped around the crystal. The time will come when the crystal must be claimed. But the magic wrapped around it will have to be unwrapped with the utmost care. That will be a quest, but not your quest or Gracie's. But you both will have a part to play." That is all he would say about it.

One morning just after breakfast, Mr. Nichols asked Chukauyon and Chawnaway to take a walk with him. He always used their new names while they were in the village. "It is time, Chawnaway." He led them far out to where the meadows began to break into foothills. Old Shep was close on his heels. A horse whinnied. It was Song of the Wind, waiting for them. "Now we shall say our good-byes," said Mr. Nichols. "But not forever, Gracie. James and I have to make a trip North to the place where the seven crystals were born. And I promised to get him home in time to do his evening chores. I shall bring him back another time. You must see each other more often now."

"Oh no!" said James. It had been weeks since he'd thought about that Sunday by the creek and getting home to do chores.

"Remember, time is different here," laughed Mr. Nichols. "You haven't been keeping track of the time, but I have."

There were tearful goodbyes. "I suppose you will be ten years older than me when I get to come back," said James.

"You never know," said Gracie, wiping her eyes. "Mr. Nichols says time is different here. Maybe you'll be the older one then."

Chapter 18

THE HIGH MOUNTAIN POOL

They rode up through the foothills until Gracie was only a tiny spot on the horizon. Then Song of the Wind took them high up in the air above the coast where water meets land. James never forgot how the waves looked rolling in and breaking on the shore. He saw now that Old Shep was right beside them, keeping up with Song of the Wind. They flew until the ocean met a long, wide river. They passed snowcapped mountains and rode over the tops of forests. Then Song of the Wind and Old Shep set down in a meadow high upon a mountain, taller than any of the other mountains. The tree line was far below them. The snow line began above them. It was sharply cool, almost cold on the meadow, though the sun was shining.

"This is the tallest mountain of the far North of the world," said Mr. Nichols. A clear pool standing at the edge of the meadow sparkled in the sunlight. "Here is where the seven crystals grew." The water was fresh and cold. It gathered from a spring flowing from rocks around it, spilling over into a small stream that wound its way through the meadow and on down the mountain. "Reach into the pool and find what you will."

James rolled up his sleeve, bent down, and looked, but the pool was so deep and blue he couldn't see anything to reach for. He put his hand in, pulling back immediately. "That's like ice!" he exclaimed. "It's too cold!"

"I didn't say it would be comfortable," said Mr. Nichols. "You must reach deeply. Never mind the cold."

"But it will freeze my arm off!" exclaimed James. His hand burned from the cold.

Mr. Nichols didn't say anything. He just waited as if he expected James to do it anyway.

James was afraid. But he took a deep breath and plunged his hand into the water until it reached his shoulder. At first he felt nothing except the burning cold. Then his hand felt a cluster of spikey rock. His fingers were so numb that he could hardly grasp it. But when he tugged, the rock gave way in his hand. He pulled it out quickly, gasping from the cold. It was a crystal rock with long, thick shards of pure, clear crystal sticking up from it in all directions. Mr. Nichols took it from him.

"Quickly now, Son," he said. "Drink from the pool."

It didn't make any sense to James. He was shaking with cold and his shirt was sopping wet all along one side. He expected that at the very least, Mr. Nichols would wrap him in a blanket. The water in the pool was colder than freezing cold, colder than inside the ice company in Sage.

"Drink all you can hold. Like this." Mr. Nichols lay down on the grass and lowered his head to the water, drinking. "Be quick about it!"

James followed, still shaking. His arm was so cold it no longer felt a part of him. He was sure his fingers would never move again. But he threw himself on the ground and drank the cold, cold water. It was colder that the coldest drink he had ever tasted. It was fresher than fresh. As he drank, warmth spread through his whole body, right down to the tips of his frozen fingers.

"This is fresher than anything you will find anywhere else," said Mr. Nichols, raising himself into a squatting position. "But not so fresh as it was the day the earth was made. Nor so healing, though a drink of this water will do you a great deal of good."

James sat up too. He was warm all over. He felt as if all the tiredness and worries he felt over almost giving the crystal to Celeste, and all the grief he felt at leaving Gracie, even his worries about Claude had dropped away from him. He unrolled his wet sleeve, exposing it to the warming sun.

Mr. Nichols took the crystal rock, holding it up to the light. The sun reflected a thousand sparkles of light. James had never seen anything so beautiful.

"Now your part is almost done, James, at least for now."

"My part?"

"Why in the Last Crystal, Son. Those who come after you will have to discover how to find it. They will need something from this crystal. Here, give me your map. They will need the map, too."

James stood, confused and unmoving.

"The map your mother gave you. You brought it with you." Mr. Nichols said. "It's in the bag on Song of the Wind's back where we left it."

James had never approached Song of the Wind alone. The horse stood fierce and proud where they had left him when they alighted. Old Shep was stretched out on the grass nearby. James was fearful. Mr. Nichols waited, unmoving. "Ask him," he said.

James nervously walked over to where the horse waited, head held high. "Song of the Wind, may I get my mother's map?" His voice trembled. "Please?"

Song of the Wind snorted and shook his mane. For a minute, James thought the horse was going to run away or maybe even bite him. But Song of the Wind took a step toward him, lowering his head, ears pointed forward. He nickered softly. Then he knelt down and rested upon the grass, waiting while James got the map from the saddlebag.

"Thank you," said James when he had the map. Song of the Wind reached out his neck and nuzzled him as if to say, "It is quite alright, glad to help." In fact, James was never entirely sure he hadn't said it.

Mr. Nichols spread out the map. "There is more to this map than your Mother knew, James. The one who claims the Last Crystal will need to be able to see it. The key to unlocking the map will come from this crystal," he said.

The rock crystal had dried in the sun. It sat on a flat rock, it's many shards sending a shower of color out in every direction. Mr. Nichols picked it up and studied the map, turning the crystal this way and that, examining each shard. "Yes," he said at last. "This one is the key."

James was overcome with curiosity. "May I look?" he asked.

"You may," said Mr. Nichols. He broke off the shard he had been looking through, handing it to him.

James tried to look through the clear shard, but he couldn't see anything at all. The marks his mother had made on the map were blurry through the crystal. "I can't see anything!"

"No. You aren't meant to. But the child who finishes the work your mother began will be able to see what she needs to see." With that he stood, throwing the crystal rock back into the pool. "Here, I will take that crystal shard and I will need to keep the map for now. We'd best be off if I'm to keep my promise. You don't want to be late and we have one more stop to make."

Song of the Wind and Old Shep were soon flying again. They went over mountains, snow, and seas before they set down in a high meadow on another mountain. A man and a boy about James' age stood waiting. They wore wide brimmed hats with a cone-shaped crown. Both had beautiful woven blankets around their shoulders. "They are expecting us," said Mr. Nichols as they dismounted. "Bring the carpetbag with you."

After what seemed a very long time with much discussion that James couldn't understand, he was asked to open the carpetbag. Following directions as Mr. Nichols guided him, he removed a beautifully decorated wooden box with a lid hinged in pure gold. It was the first time he had seen it. The box was a work of art in itself. The boy held out a colorful blanket, woven in an intricate design. Mr. Nichols motioned for James to put the box in the blanket.

James hesitated for a moment. He had an almost overwhelming desire to open the box and have a look. They waited. Nobody said anything.

Now that he had the box, what was to prevent him from having a look? After all, if a child could open the Alabaster Box, could a child not open this box? He wasn't that much older than his mother had been. She had opened the Alabaster Box and this very wooden box.

Something in him also resisted. It was like a voice urging him to hand over the box. James broke out in a sweat. He gritted his teeth. Exerting all of his will power, he put the box in the blanket. When he let go, he breathed a sigh of relief. The boy wrapped the blanket around it.

Mr. Nichols said something to the man and boy, then turned to James. "This man is the Keeper of the Crystal. He and his son will keep it safe for us. It is a task he agreed to some time ago, for I have long guessed that the crystal must be hidden away in time. Celeste gave up her ability to return to times before when she became a mortal. But the crystal is still bound by her power. If anyone opens the wooden box, time will be of little consequence. She will know. But she can't touch the box while it is here. Breaking the power binding the crystal is a job for another day. Our work is done for now. We shall take you home."

When Song of the Wind set down along the creek near James' house, it was almost time to bring in the cows.

"There's something I don't understand," said James as he dismounted. "Why did my mother have to take the Last Crystal in the first place?"

"She didn't," said Mr. Nichols. "But she is the one who unlocked the first part of the mystery of how to undo the magic."

"Why did it have to be her?"

"I don't know," said Mr. Nichols as he dismounted. "Perhaps it didn't. Perhaps it just happened."

"Why was Celeste able to have my Mamma and Daddy killed? Because she did that, didn't she? Why couldn't you save them, too?"

"I don't know that, either. I got there in time to save you and Gracie."

"Will Celeste leave us alone now?" asked James.

"I will take care of Celeste," said Mr. Nichols.

"I wish she were dead!" James blurted out. "Ruby and Junior Swathmore, too. I wish they were all dead." He felt a deep fury welling up inside, ready to burst out like a raging fire.

"Understandably." Mr. Nichols said calmly, putting his arm around James. "The hardest thing you have to do is not over, James. Forgiveness isn't something to take lightly. You may not ever be able to forgive Celeste or Ruby and Junior. But try and live toward forgiveness. It will shelter you from hatred. Hatred destroys." He lightly swung onto Song of the Wind's back. "I'll see you next summer. You can spend the summer with Gracie—in between chores." His eyes twinkled with merriment. Waving as Song of the Wind wheeled, he rode away across the pasture. James watched, holding on to Old Shep as Mr. Nichols disappeared over the hill.

The cows were all waiting for him to lead them home. Old Shep stayed close by. The fire of anger gradually dissipated as he led the cows back to the barn for milking.

That evening at supper, Mama asked, "Well James, did you find enough to amuse yourself this afternoon?"

"I had a great time. I lived in an Indian village and flew on a horse to the highest mountain in the far north of the world," said James. "And Old Shep went with me."

"Sounds like more than a day's work," said Papa, eyes twinkling.

"I hope you never outgrow that imagination," said Mama, giving him a kiss on the head before she set the last dish on the table.

"Me too," said James.

Chapter 19

WAR

The maid brought Celeste a post card. She smiled triumphantly as she saw the address in her own handwriting. Her face fell, though when she read the message: "The boy doesn't have it. Leave him alone. I've taken it where you will never be able to find it. It isn't too late to change your mind. Your devoted brother, C'lestin."

That is what you think, she thought. He still didn't understand the magic that bound the crystals. *It isn't over yet, brother dearest.*

"Somethin' troublin' you, Lovely?" Teddy Mack asked as they sat down to dinner later that evening.

"Don't bother ordering those moths," she said. "I've changed my mind."

***

169

Claude dropped out of school. Mr. Tipton said his father had a broken leg. So Claude had to take over work on the farm. James wanted to be sorry, but he couldn't. When Claude was at school, not a day passed that he didn't do something to try and get his goat. Claude didn't punch him anymore but he tried to turn the other boys against him and constantly taunted him. He was so sneaky that Mr. Tipton never saw.

Mama went by the Higgins place with a couple of loaves of her wheat bread right after they heard Mr. Higgins had been injured. But Mrs. Higgins wouldn't let her in the house. "She told me Mr. Higgins won't hear to charity," Mama reported. "I said it wasn't charity. It's what any neighbor would do. I asked if we could help out in any way. But she refused. She just shut the door on me."

"Their wheat is looking good," said Papa. "I don't see how Claude is going to be able to handle things by himself now that the older boys have all enlisted in the army."

"The thing is," said Mama, "Norma Jean Bates was over yesterday with baked beans and she let her in."

"I guess we know what that's about," said Papa. James knew it had to do with being German. He guessed Mrs. Higgins didn't know that Mrs. Bates grew up in a German-American family.

Winter came and went. Claude didn't come back to school. They saw him in town with his father. Mr. Higgins was walking now, but he had a bad limp and used one crutch.

There was more news of war. April came. President Wilson asked the U.S. Congress to declare war on Germany. Mama and Papa read the papers in worried silence. Young men whose families could spare them volunteered for the army. There was more war talk at school.

People were asked to buy war bonds to support the war. Papa refused. He said he would not do anything to support war. It was a matter of conscience. When word got out, James began to hear more ugly talk at school. Even at church, some families who had always been friendly before, cut them cold. Papa said there are ways to love your country without fighting. A lot of people didn't feel that way.

Mr. Tipton said that standing up for what you believe isn't cowardly, even if it means you aren't fighting. It was hard for kids at school to accept that. It was hard for James hear them call his Papa a coward. He wanted to smash somebody. But he didn't. It was a relief when school came to an end.

"This is terrible," said Mama one afternoon. She was reading the paper. "There's an article here about President Wilson's Flag Day Speech. Let me read what he said, 'The military masters of Germany have filled our unsuspecting communities with vicious spies and conspirators and have sought to corrupt the opinion of our people.' If things weren't bad enough," she sighed. "Now people are going to think that we aren't just cowards, but 'vicious spies,' who have been living here just so we can undermine the government and send war secrets to the Kaiser. It doesn't give his full speech. I'm disappointed in President Wilson, though."

Papa rolled his eyes. "It won't matter what the President said. They'll take it and use it for their own purposes. Religious freedom doesn't mean anything to some people. For them freedom means freedom for everybody to believe the same thing and act the same way."

One day Papa returned from Cedar Hills empty handed. He'd gone in to buy feed for the chickens. The feed store refused to do business with him. "There was a sign that says, 'If you didn't buy war bonds, don't buy from us," he said. "I went in anyway. Jim Perkins was behind the counter, so I figured he'd be reasonable. He took one look at me and said, 'Can't you read, Matthias?' and turned his back on me."

"We've traded with him for years!" said Mama, disbelieving.

"I ran into Alf Yoder on the way out of Town. He said the German-speaking church is going to have to close," said Papa. "Seems that even speaking German is suspect now."

"Why do these people think our ancestors left Germany in the first place?" said Mama. "They wanted to be free to worship in their own way they and they didn't want to fight in Germany's wars!"

"Think. That's the key word. They aren't thinking. They're just reacting." Papa sighed. "Anyway, we can't fix it by fretting. I reckon I'll have to see if I can buy enough corn from last year's crop to tide us over. Paul Davis was selling earlier this year. James, what if we go over in the morning and see about it?"

James could tell they were in for a hot day when they hitched up the team the next morning. They took the wagon, hoping to return with corn. If so, they'd take it straight to Bates Mill to have it ground into chicken feed.

"Won't be long before the wheat is ready," said Papa, looking over the wheat fields along both sides of the road. It had been a dry spring. Now everybody hoped that rain would hold off another week or so until after harvest. As they came to the corner where the road to the Higgins farm cut off, they saw a column of dark black smoke billowing up into the air.

"That doesn't look right," said Papa. "That smoke is moving too fast. We'd better go see. If a fire gets out of control in this weather it could do some real damage."

He set the horses to a gallop. As they got to the Higgins place they could see that the smoke was rising from a line of flames moving up one side of the hill behind the house.

"That's headed for their wheat!" yelled James.

"Looks like maybe a trash fire got out of control," said Papa. "Thank God it's moving away from the house."

They could see Claude frantically hitching the plow. "Good, he's going to plow between the wheat and the fire. He's going to need some help." Mr. Higgins and his wife were shoveling dirt, throwing it on the fire. But the fire was gaining ground. Papa pulled in the yard, jumped out of the wagon and began unhitching their two horses. He didn't ask if he could help, he just went to work. "You take a horse and ride over to the Davis place as fast as you can, James. Tell Earl and his Papa. I'll see if there is another plow I can hitch up to this horse. They're going to need that fire strip fast if they're going to keep it out of the wheat."

As James rode away, he could see Papa taking the reins from Claude and pointing to their horse. Claude wasn't arguing, either.

James felt the urgency of getting help. But part of him thought that if the Higgins wheat burned, it was because they deserved it. Mr. Higgins had been downright mean to Papa and Claude was unbearable. He knew what Papa would say, though. "Doesn't matter how other folk act. It's the right thing to do."

He urged his horse on, going as fast as he could go. If they didn't get that fire under control, everybody on this side of the creek could lose their wheat.

Chapter 20

FIGHTING FIRE WITH FIRE

The Davis place was about half a mile up the road from the turn off to the Higgins place. The wind was blowing in the wrong direction, so they hadn't seen the smoke when James got there. Earl and his Daddy dropped what they were doing and threw a couple of shovels and all the buckets they had in their wagon. "We'll start a bucket brigade from the stock tank," yelled Mr. Davis. "We'll need every hand we can get." Mrs. Davis and Earl's younger brothers and sister ran out to get in the wagon. "You ride on back and make sure the windmill is on and pumping water, James. We'll be there as fast as we can."

When James got back to the Higgins place, it looked like the fire was winning. It had already burned more than half way up the hill. Papa and Claude were both plowing a fire strip, at the crest

176

of the hill where the grass extended the length of the wheat field. But the ground was dry. It was hard going.

James went straight to the windmill and turned it on, bringing more water into the stock tank. There were two buckets by the pump. He filled them from the tank and started up the hill, not waiting for the Davis wagon. "Leave the fire!" yelled Papa. "Water down the wheat along the edge of the field. It will slow things down if the fire leaps the barrier."

When the Davis family arrived they didn't ask what to do. They formed a line going up the hill to the wheat. Mrs. Davis dipped and handed a bucket to their girl, who ran with it to one of the boys, who ran with it to the next boy, then to James who ran it the rest of the way up the hill to the wheat and brought it back empty for the next. It was slow work. He emptied bucket after bucket of water along the edge of the wheat field.

Meanwhile, Mr. Davis and Earl took their shovels and joined Mr. and Mrs. Higgins. They worked in front of the fire, throwing dirt on the flames. They'd kept it from sweeping the entire hill, saving the house. But they hadn't stopped it. The fire made a long, licking wall that stretched diagonally up the hill. It moved steadily toward the wheat field above.

The wind picked up, sending the fire along at an alarming speed. James took another full bucket, turning to go back up the hill. He'd lost count of the number. All of a sudden Papa dropped the reins of the horse and stepped in his path, throwing his straw hat down. "Pour it on me, Son!" he ordered, tying his pocket handkerchief over his face. "Quick! Get that other bucket, too. Now take the reins," he ordered after James had splashed him all over a second time. "Keep that bucket brigade going," he said to Davis boy. Then he ran toward the fire.

When James saw what his father was doing, his heart nearly stopped. Whipped by the fire, the flames had reached out in uneven fingers grabbing at the dry grass and weeds. Mr. Higgins was working too close to the flame. His leg was weak from the break he'd had. He took a tumble and couldn't get up. Before he could drag himself out of the way, the flames surrounded him. He was trapped by a wall of flame. He threw off his straw hat. The wind caught it, sending it up in flames where it landed on the other side of the fire strip. It licked against the wet wheat. Earl's little brother got to it, dousing it with water before it could ignite the wheat. Papa had been right about wetting down the wheat.

Papa stepped into the fire, lifted Mr. Higgins up, and carried him out. Rolling him over in the dirt, he and Mrs. Higgins put out the flames that had caught on his clothing. James couldn't believe his Papa could lift somebody that much heavier. Mr. Higgins was burned, but not as badly as he might have been, thanks to Papa's quick thinking. Papa was singed, but unharmed, thanks to his wet clothes.

James guided the plow. Papa picked up Mr. Higgins' shovel the minute Mr. Higgins was able to lean on Mrs. Higgins and walk. Papa began digging and throwing dirt on the fire, leaving him to plow with Claude. He and Claude seemed to be fighting a losing battle. The ground was so dry the plow barely scraped it. When he lowered the plow the horse had to go so slow they made little progress.

Mrs. Higgins and Paul Davis helped Mr. Higgins down the hill where she could dress the burns. She put him under an elm tree, propping up his leg. The leg was injured, but he hadn't broken it again. He could watch, though he was helpless to do anything else. She came back to join in the digging again once she'd taken care of his burns.

The Taylor family came. They had buckets, spades and a plow in their wagon. They'd seen the smoke. Mrs. Taylor, Jess, Frank and their two sisters joined the bucket brigade, speeding it up considerably. Mr. Taylor hitched up their plow to one of their horses. He went to work helping Claude and James while the oldest boy went to work with a spade, throwing dirt on the flames.

Still the fire came. Where they managed to extinguish the flames with dirt in one place, it seemed to break out in two others until it covered the length of the hill and went into the pasture behind the Higgins barn and corn crib.

"Claude," yelled Papa, "With this wind, we're not going to be able to make that strip wide enough to keep the fire from jumping it to the wheat when it gets up there. Any change in direction and I'm afraid it will put the barn in danger. I think we'd better start a back-fire. It's risky. What do you think? I'm not sure your Pa can make that decision now."

His face white with panic, Claude said, "I don't know."

"I think it's a good idea, Claude," yelled Mr. Taylor. He sent Jess running down to ask Mr. Higgins. Mr. Higgins had passed out when Papa pulled him from the fire. Now he was conscious and seemed to understand. Jess signaled thumbs up and they set to work making a back-fire. Papa issued orders like he was a general in the army. When it came to fighting fire, he wasn't a pacifist.

"Get the bucket brigade over here to wet the grass along the fire strip," he yelled. "That'll help keep it from going the wrong direction. We need another brigade to wet down that grass along the fence around the barn, too." Mr. Davis got two bucket lines going. Everybody pitched in. They poured water all along the strip ahead of the fire headed toward the wheat and behind the fire along the barnyard fence. They left a wide swath of grass to start the back-fire. Now there wasn't much distance between the fire and the strip he and Claude had plowed.

"Hurry," yelled Papa. "The wind's in our favor." They started the back-fire ahead of the wall of fire. Fanning it, they watched it gain momentum as the wind whipped it along. It moved toward the fire that was fast taking the whole hill. A wide swath of scorched earth scarred the land where it had been. The two walls of fire meet. A cheer went up from everyone as they watched the fire burn itself out.

"Let's keep the bucket brigade going," yelled Papa. Every spare hand was devoted to throwing water or dirt along the fire line to make sure the fire was thoroughly extinguished.

Just then Norma Jean Bates and Patsy drove up in their wagon. Mama and Maggie were with them. Maggie sat on Patsy's lap. Norma Jean had just finished getting dinner ready when she saw the smoke. She threw everything into her wagon, stopping for Mama.

"She said it looked like a run-away fire and people would need something to eat, so I threw in few things," said Mama. A few things meant their dinner: a roast chicken, lambs quarter cooked with ham, coleslaw, scalloped potatoes, two jars of homemade pickled beets she threw in for good measure, two apple pies and a loaf of gingerbread. Mrs. Bates had enough for a small army, too: friend chicken, green beans, potato salad, applesauce and two angel food cakes. She suggested they set up a picnic in the back of the wagon, pulling it up closer to the house.

"Mr. Bates will wonder happened to his dinner," she laughed. "But he'll say it was for a good cause. He won't be able to complain about left-overs for supper, either. I left him a note. He may be along directly."

Mrs. Taylor left the bucket brigade now that the fire was under control and she could be spared. She helped out with the food.

Mrs. Higgins hurried back and forth to the kitchen adding a pot roast and homemade rolls to the feast. She apologized that there hadn't been time to make a full dinner.

"But that's why we're here," said Norma Jean Bates. "Of course you haven't had time to finish getting dinner. You've been fighting a fire, for goodness sake."

After awhile Papa and the other men agreed that the fire was out and there were no dangerous sparks smoldering among the ashes. The remaining members of the bucket brigade all washed up in the stock tank. "Reckon it was a good thing you came along when you did," said Mr. Higgins when the men joined the group near the wagon. He sat with his leg propped up, looking at Papa, but he didn't look him in the eye. "We saved the crop."

"Reckon you'd have done the same," said Papa. James wasn't so sure. Part of him was proud and relieved that they'd saved the wheat, part of him still wished the whole field had burned. But Papa couldn't hear his thoughts. He kept right on talking to Mr. Higgins. "Thank God we happened to be on our way past. Your son did a man's work out there."

Claude was carrying a block of ice from the icebox so they could have iced tea with their dinner. "Damn well should have," said Mr. Higgins. "Wouldn't have started if he hadn't been lookin' the other way when he was supposed to be watchin' the trash fire. Ought to give him a good thrashin'."

James could see Claude's face go red. Papa said, "It could have happened to anybody. That wind came up out of nowhere. Anyway, I reckon he's had punishment enough."

It was an awkward moment. Norma Jean Bates quickly intervened. "Let's thank the Lord for the work everybody's done saving our neighbor's wheat, and have some dinner." She asked Papa to say the prayer. Nobody had to be asked twice when it was time to eat.

James and all the boys ate together, sitting under one of the trees. Claude didn't say anything to him. He didn't say much to anybody. Later James saw Papa pat Claude on the back, and say something to him.

When James went to refill his plate, Paul Davis was standing nearby. Papa came up.

"By the way, Paul, James and I were on our way over to your place when we saw the fire. We wanted to see if we could buy some corn for chicken feed. We couldn't get any in town yesterday."

"I was just over there yesterday mornin', Karl," said Mr. Davis. "They couldn't have run out."

"Oh, I think they had plenty of chicken feed," said Papa. "They just didn't think I was patriotic enough to buy from them."

Mr. Davis snorted in disgust. "I'm out of corn. But tell you what. Take half of my chicken feed. Next time I'll buy for you when I pick up feed. We won't change their minds over there, but we can get around them."

"Thanks," said Papa. "That means a lot."

"You kiddin'?" said Mr. Davis. "How long have we known each other, Karl? There's lots of things we don't agree on, but treatin' folk right isn't one of them."

"Higgins isn't going to be able to bring that wheat in by himself," said Papa. "We're going to have to get together and help Claude. I hope he'll let us do it."

"He won't cotton to much you have to say," said Mr. Davis. "I saw how he didn't look you in the eye when he thanked you. But he did thank you in his own way. I'll grant him that. He has a lot of bad feelings about Germans. That's not likely to change. Leave this to me."

Everybody had seconds. Mrs. Taylor and Mama set out the pie. Mrs. Higgins had made enough coffee and iced tea for an army, too.

Mr. Bates rode up just as people started in on the pie. He went straight to Mr. Higgins. "I'd shake your hand if it wasn't all bandaged up. Looks like you all got this thing under control. I saw the smoke just about the time I was leavin' the mill for dinner. I saw the Missus' note and came right over. Thank the good Lord it is out now."

"Never knowed folk to be so helpful," said Mr. Higgins. "I sure appreciate it."

"We're a community, Higgins. We work together," said Mr. Bates.

"What are you talkin' about, Bates," teased Mr. Taylor. "We work together. You ride up in time for pie!" Everyone had a good laugh.

Mr. Davis, who had planted himself next to the pie, said in a loud voice. "Since I'm surrounded by neighbors, this is a good time to bring up a problem. My wheat will be ready for cuttin' in a day or two. I know some of you hire those groups that follow the harvest up from Texas, but I can't afford to do that this year. If any of you can help me get my combine workin', and give me a hand at bringin' in my wheat, I'm more than glad to cut yours in exchange for the labor. I've kept that combine runnin' with bailin' wire and chewin' gum for years. This sure isn't the year to be gettin' parts."

"Sounds like a good plan to me," said Papa. "I'm in."

"I haven't been able to get parts either, Davis," said Mr. Taylor. "That sounds like a stroke of genius. Maybe between the two of us we can put together one good machine. Me and the boys can pitch in on your place if you help on ours. And you can use our horses to pull."

"I'll help," said Claude.

"I'll help, too, if I'm on my feet," said Mr. Higgins.

After James went to bed that night, he wanted a drink of water. So he went to the kitchen. Mama and Papa were in the living room talking. He didn't mean to eavesdrop, but he couldn't help hearing.

"Claude wasn't responsible for that fire getting away," said Mama. "He took the blame."

"I know," said Papa. "I could see it in his eyes."

"Well, Elsie Higgins told me it was her fault," said Mama. "She thanked me for what you did. She even apologized for not letting me in the other day. She said Dale Higgins can be a hard man. It was hard for him to accept that a German saved his life. Maybe it will get him to thinking. He did more or less say 'thank you'. I think that was a big step for him."

"I don't know, Hannalore," said Papa.

"Another thing," said Mama. "We never see Elsie Higgins out and about. I don't think he lets her off the place. She has some pretty bad bruises, too. Hazel Taylor made a comment and Elsie said she ran into a chair. But I think he is beating up on her."

"It shows some good in Claude, trying to protect her," said Papa.

"Isn't there anything we can do?" asked Mama.

"Getting people working together to bring in the wheat will help," said Papa. "Maybe you can organize the women to get dinner for the crews at each place. When you eat together and work together it is hard to hold on to a grudge. We can't make Dale Higgins do right, but we can give him the chance to."

"I'll talk to Norma Jean tomorrow," said Mama. "Maybe if Elsie gets out with some of the other women, she'll build up her courage. She shouldn't have to put up with him beating on her."

Papa sighed. "I'd like to think people can change, Hannalore. But Higgins is a powder keg, just waiting for somebody to come along with a match."

Chapter 21

Sweet Butterhorns 2 for 1¢

TAKING A STAND

Harvest came and went. Paul Davis' plan worked. Not only did it help the Higgins family, but everybody else who took part said it changed harvest from one of the hardest times of the year to one of the best. Mr. Higgins wasn't able to help. But Claude showed up and worked at all five farms.

Mama and Norma Jean Bates asked Elsie Higgins to help organize the dinners served at noon. They set up like they had after the Higgins fire, using the back of a wagon. Norma Jean Bates got Mr. Higgins to drive the team of horses pulling the dinner wagon, as they called it. It was an important job. They made him feel like they needed a man to do it. "It is possibly even more important than driving the horses pulling the combine," said Norma Jean when she recruited

Mr. Higgins. Later, she explained to Mama, "It's not that we couldn't do it ourselves, Hannalore, but some men think women can't do anything without their help. It burns me up, but it is worth the deception if it helps Elsie."

James, Earl Davis and the Taylor boys all worked alongside Claude. In the end, James wouldn't have said they were all friends. But at least they got the work done without any name-calling or threats. For James, that was a minor miracle.

James noticed that Papa took every opportunity he could to encourage Claude. Papa wasn't a big one for compliments. He made a point to thank Claude, though, giving him a pat on the back now and then and showing respect for his ideas. That was how Papa treated everyone. He didn't heap them with praise; he just encouraged and respected people.

That summer, after harvest and the plowing were done, James and his family had to go in to Cedar Hills and swear their loyalty to the U.S. government. Cedar Hills was the County Seat where the Court House, jail, and county government offices were located. "I expect every other German-American family in the whole county will be there," said Papa as he brought the horses to a halt near the Court House." James didn't know anybody who was there except Mr. and Mrs. Yoder.

Chapter 21

The Yoders owned the bakery in Town. Papa used to stop in and buy rye bread made by an old German recipe. Mrs. Yoder usually gave James a *hörnchen*. They didn't sell *hörnchen* anymore, at least not by that name. They sold sweet butter horn rolls. People didn't buy things with German names on them. As far as James was concerned, they were his favorite no matter what you called them.

A small crowd of people stood on either side of the steps to the Court House to watch families go in. "Dirty Krauts!" yelled one man who hadn't any business calling anybody dirty. His overalls looked like they had enough dirt in them to stand up by themselves. "Spies! Traitors!" shrieked a woman's voice from somewhere in the crowd. "Go back where you came from!" The ugly comments all ran together. The Deputy Sherriff stood guard. He blew a whistle and pointed to a man who was carrying a gunny sack. "If you've got what I think you have in that bag, you'd better be gettin' ready to make soup. If I see a single tomato or cabbage flyin' through the air you gonna enjoy a night on the county, Buddy. I'll lock you in myself."

Once inside, everybody had to say the pledge to the flag and sing "The Star Spangled Banner" together. People checked to see that they knew the words, too. "You there, what's that you're mublin'?" one of the interrogators asked, pointing to a frightened woman just behind James. "Step out here. Let's hear you sing 'The Star Spangled Banner' nice and clear."

The poor woman shook with fright. She sang in a halting voice. When she finished, the interrogator, an enormous man with a belly that hung over his trousers, said. "What about the second verse?"

Somebody behind James in the group of German-Americans said very calmly, "Sir, if you can sing it, I'm sure she'll be glad to."

"Who said that!" demanded the man.

"That's enough, Logan," said one of the other interrogators. "Nobody knows the second verse. Wouldn't be fair. It ain't like it's the national anthem anyway."

"If it ain't, it oughta be," muttered Logan.

James heard his mother breath a sign of relief. The woman stepped back down, still shaking all over. Mr. Logan made several people sing the first verse. Then the adults all had to step up and sign a paper swearing loyalty to the United States.

The Deputy Sherriff had to clear a path on the Court House steps when it was time to leave. As they walked through the crowd, a lady yelled, "Proves nothin' you Kaiser-lovin' Krauts!"

"Yeah," called a man. "The very devil himself could sing 'The Star Spangled Banner' if you put him to it."

After that there was so much shouting, James couldn't make out what was being said. Signing oaths did little to reassure those who were on the lookout for traitors anyway.

The local newspaper, "The Cedar Hills News Dispatch," reported on the new draft law. "What the Allies need most is fresh troops. The Selective Service Act, signed into law by President Wilson on May 18, 1917, requires all men in the US between the ages of 21 and 30 to register for military service." The article reported that the first group of US Citizens to be drafted into the army were reporting for duty. "Cedar Hills is doing its part to support the war effort as our finest young men report to serve."

Most of the German-Americans in the county who were drafted reported to serve in the army like everybody else. Most of the time, other soldiers welcomed them. Sometimes they were ridiculed.

It was really hard for pacifists, like Mama and Papa, though. Some pacifists refused to report for service when they were drafted. They were not only ridiculed, but many were thrown in jail. Not all pacifists were German-Americans. But it was even worse for German-American pacifists who were drafted and refused to join the army.

Papa was past the draft age, but he felt the effects anyway.

Tension between German-Americans and other folk mounted. Sometimes stores, like the feed store in Cedar Hills, wouldn't sell to them. Gates and fence posts of German-Americans were painted yellow in the night. People called names, and worse.

Mama said an article in the "Dispatch" warned that anybody born in Germany or Austria should be considered a spy unless there was proof that they weren't. "Really?" snorted Papa, when she read the article aloud to them. "So what happened to the principle of innocent until proven guilty? And what happened to the first amendment to the Constitution of the United States and the fourteenth amendment?"

Congress shall make no law respecting an establishment of religion, James repeated the first amendment to himself. He'd had to learn the whole thing by heart. The first amendment guaranteed freedom of religion, freedom of speech, freedom of the press, and freedom for people to gather peacefully and to petition their government. He didn't know the fourteenth amendment by heart, but he knew that it was passed after the Civil War to guarantee equal protection under the law and citizen rights.

Newspapers reported that Red Cross bandages had been damaged by German spies who poured chemicals and crushed glass on them.

Nobody had been arrested. One article said that German submarines were landing with the help of German-Americans who flashed signals to them from shore. There wasn't any proof of any of these claims. Some people said the government wasn't trying hard enough to catch the spies or there would be proof. Other people said they didn't care whether there was proof or not, it was probably true.

Even the "Dispatch" was filled with letters to the editor demanding that more be done to find and arrest German spies living in their midst. Papa and Mama no longer went into Cedar Hills to get supplies. They bought all their groceries in MacLean's General Store. Paul Davis picked up chicken and livestock feed for them. Mama sent money with Norma Jean Bates to do back-to-school shopping for James. Last-year's shirts came well above his wrists now. Mrs. Bates shopped for anything Mama needed and couldn't find in Sage.

The County Fair opened again. James didn't have an exhibit this year. But Amos Counts did. His pig won a blue ribbon and first prize at the county fair. Mr. Tipton announced that Amos would be absent during the State Fair. James clapped louder than anybody.

Mr. Tipton announced they'd be collecting peach pits and walnut shells for the Red Cross. "The Germans are using chlorine gas. Lives can be saved with gas masks made with charcoal from peach pits or walnut shells. It takes two hundred peach pits or two pounds of nutshells to make enough charcoal for one gas mask. Schools all across America are having contests to see who can gather the most peach pits and walnut shells. Sage can do its part. Maybe this is a way we can all help."

When James told Mama and Papa about it that evening, Papa said, "James, that is a hard one. I believe in saving life. But are the masks going to make it possible for soldiers to take more lives? What do you think about it?"

"I'd like to help out," said James. "It isn't like buying war bonds where the money can go to anything. It's to keep people from being killed. Sometimes the wind takes the gas over villages and everybody is killed. Mr. Tipton said it is a terrible way to die. Besides if the Germans see that they can't kill our soldiers by using gas, they won't use it and it won't kill innocent people who aren't even fighting."

"Then I'll support you, Son," said Papa. "What do you say, Hannalore?" Mama agreed.

One afternoon a buggy pulled up in the yard. It was Alf and Bertha Yoder. She brought James a bag of sweet butter horn rolls.

Alf Yoder got right down to brass tacks. "It is getting dangerous for us pacifists in Cedar Hills. Since the German-speaking church had to close, we've been having an English service in the

Methodist Church on Sunday evenings. Pastor Newkirk, the Methodist minister, says there are folks putting pressure on the church to shut us down. Being pacifist is equal to being a spy as far as some of these people are concerned. Pastor Newkirk is in a hard spot. He says they won't give in to that kind of hooliganism, but we don't want to endanger anybody. Over by Bingley, the Mennonite pastor was tarred and feathered by an angry crowd just last week."

Mama gasped. "James, maybe you should take Maggie and. . ."

"No, Hannalore," interrupted Papa. "James needs to hear this. We're all in it together."

So James stayed, wondering what being tarred and feathered actually meant. It sounded like something awful. He hadn't forgotten Claude's threat that time the boys all jumped him.

"We don't feel safe in our own country!" said Mrs. Yoder.

"So far there hasn't been anything like that here," said Mama. "But James has been bullied at school and there are some folk at church who don't speak to us anymore."

"We're the only German-American family left around Sage," said Papa. "There used to be a small group, but families left to find work in the City or farms sold over the years. Others, like Norma Jean Bates, married into other families. Folk know us. We grew up here."

"It's getting hard in town," said Mrs. Yoder. "Since the Espionage Act was passed, everything we do and say is taken as obstruction of the war effort. God forbid that anybody should walk into our house unannounced and hear us speaking German."

"You can't even say anything critical of the war effort," said Papa. "Not unless you want to fork over $10,000 for violating the Espionage Act. Those are tactics of a dictatorship."

"We are losing our first amendment rights," said Mama. "Who would have thought we could come to such a day in the United States?"

"Our Sherriff is behind us one hundred percent," said Mr. Yoder. "At least we have that to be grateful for. But what we came to ask is whether you'd be willing to shelter families who need to get out of Cedar Hills—if it comes to that. We got to talking after church Sunday night and decided we'd better have plans to protect our families. "

"Of course," said Papa. He looked at Mama. "We don't even have to think about it, do we, Hannalore?"

"It could be dangerous," said Mr. Yoder. "Several folk from the church work over at the Cotton Gin in Town. At the Gin they've had to make an office for a member of the American Protective League so he can watch the German-Americans to make sure they aren't committing acts of sabotage."

"You don't mean it!" said Mama. "I've been keeping up with things in the paper, but I missed that. And truthfully, we haven't been into town for almost a year—not since Jim Perkins refused to do business with Karl."

"They look in at the bakery regularly," Mr. Yoder continued. "I have to fly the American flag now. I don't object to the flag. Actually, I like the idea. I never had thought about flying one over the bakery before. I run the flag up every morning now. So far I still have a good business, thank God."

"From what I've been reading, the Protective League is trying to track down German-American families who have changed their names," said Papa. "People like Norma Jean Bates—one of our neighbors—will be identified as a suspicious Germans. They're watching everybody."

"We're being watched, all right," said Mrs. Yoder. "There is a man who regularly comes in the shop and buys one roll. His head is going around like an owl's, trying to see if there is something suspicious going on. I can't imagine what he expects to find."

"Buying war bonds is becoming a bigger issue than ever," said Mr. Yoder. "I have somebody on me about that nearly every day now. There is some hope, though. A group of pacifists are trying to get President Wilson to agree to a compromise for our young men who are drafted. Right now, if they refuse the draft they can be put in prison or sent to an internment camp. We're hoping that there will be some kind of alternative service that benefits humanity, but not the war."

Mama served up coffee and cherry pie. It was one of James' favorites. Mr. Yoder liked it, too. "That's mighty fine pie. You could put us out of business, Mrs. Matthias!" Mama beamed under the praise.

Later, the Yoders got ready to take their leave. "We appreciate what you're willing to do," said Mr. Yoder. "You do understand that it might be risky."

"Yes," said Mama. "Karl is right. We're glad to provide shelter if it's needed. We're out here where it's safe. This is a way we can help."

"As you say, we're taking our stand," said Papa.

"Shouldn't we have an escape plan?" asked James as the Yoder buggy pulled away. Mr. Yoder had talked about it.

"I don't think so," said Papa. "Nobody is going to come looking for us out here."

"Karl, I think James is right," said Mama. "God forbid we'll need one, but if anybody has to take sanctuary here, we ought to have an agreed upon plan about how we get them out of the house and where we meet up. There could be people from town coming for them. It would be wrong for us to sit here imagining it couldn't happen."

Chapter 22

THE COLT

Celeste's yearling colt grew into a fine two-year-old. It placed in the Kentucky Derby, but didn't do well at Belmont, or the Preakness. She was disappointed, but then, she'd let Teddy Mack pick him out. Teddy Mack promised her another trip to the great horse show and a new colt. It rankled her to go back to the horse show, knowing they were that close to Sage and James Matthias, who had so deceived her.

How her brother, C'lestin got involved in the business was a mystery. He was like that, showing up at the wrong time. She knew that the post card he sent was to be believed. It was just like him to remember that as a mortal, she could only move forward in time. He *was always a stickler for the rules,* she thought resentfully. He'd taken the crystal back to some earlier century and hidden it. He didn't say so, but he didn't have to tell Celeste for her to know. They'd been too close when they were young. She knew how he thought.

There was something she was pretty sure he didn't account for. It gave her wicked satisfaction. The crystal was still bound to the magic she had placed around it when she was an Immortal. If he opened the first of the two boxes holding the crystal, he would die. She wouldn't have admitted it, even to herself. But Celeste hoped that he knew better than to try.

If C'lestin tried to get at the crystal, he'd have to use a child. And if a child opened the first box, she would know regardless of whether the boxes were opened in the past or present. Time could not limit the magic. She hadn't any magical power left except for the power that was tied to the crystal, but there might be a way to use the magic to send a child back into time to get the crystal for her. It was worth considering.

She'd been too busy to do much considering. Teddy Mack took her to Hollywood to have a look at all the new things going on there. It gave Celeste great satisfaction to upstage stars of silent film and the theater. Several producers begged her to let them do screen tests, but she would have none of it. Her beauty was above such trivialization.

As they made the drive from their ranch near Dallas to Oklahoma City for the horse show, she kept thinking about James. *How dare he give the postcard to my brother? The little sneak. And after Teddy Mack bought so many cattle from the Matthias herd!* She couldn't think of a punishment severe enough for James.

"What are you brooding about now, Lovely?" asked Teddy Mack.

Sometimes Teddy Mack got uncomfortably close to what she was thinking. "I was just thinking of that family we bought the herd from."

"Don't know as I'd call three yearling calves a herd," said Teddy Mack, oblivious to the seething going on inside Celeste. "You took a real shine to that boy. I thought you were getting' him that fancy butterfly from Africa."

"No. I was just trying to show an interest. Children bore me. That's why I told you not to order the moths. I didn't want to get too involved."

"Whatever you say, Lovely. They seemed like a nice family to me."

Celeste took an unusual interest in the exhibits at the fair. She carefully read the names of each exhibitor. Teddy Mack was surprised when she wanted to see all the livestock on exhibit, even the pigs, but he usually went along with what she wanted. She didn't tell him, but someone said there was an entry from Sage, a pig. A wicked idea was forming.

It wasn't as smelly in the pig barn as she expected. Fortunately, the exhibit from Sage was easily found. Best of all, the boy was by himself. There were no encumbering adults around to mess up her plan. It wasn't necessary to send Teddy Mack on an errand or to hypnotize the boy, either. Setting her wicked plan in motion was as easy as taking candy from a baby.

"I'm no judge of pigs, but I'd say that is an excellent pig," said Celeste when they came to where Amos Counts had his pig penned up.

"Yes m'am," said Amos, standing politely.

"For sure. That's a mighty fine pig, young man," said Teddy Mack.

"Thank you, Sir," said Amos, beaming.

"I notice you are from Sage," said Celeste sweetly, projecting as if she were an actor standing on the stage of a huge theater. "There was a boy who exhibited from Sage last year, I believe."

"James Matthias," said Amos. "And he got to go to the Best of Show, too."

"Yes, we met him. Whatever became of him?" Celeste asked. She was sure her voice carried out into the exhibit shed. "I understand that German-American families are under suspicion with the war going on."

"Not the Matthias family," said Amos. "Everybody in Sage knows them."

"Oh dear," said Celeste loudly, in her most sympathetic tone. "They are the most dangerous ones, aren't they? Planted by the Kaiser and just waiting to betray the rest of us?"

Amos' eyes looked like they would pop out of his head. He didn't know what to say.

Teddy Mack didn't give him a chance. "What are you talkin' about, Celeste? That is just plain horse manure! You were married to a German Count."

She smiled at him indulgently. "So I was. But then I found you, didn't I?" She didn't need to say more. Her wicked plan had begun its work. It wasn't Amos Counts she was depending on, either. She had shrewdly observed that there were two entries from Cedar Hills in the live-stock barn. She remembered passing through Cedar Hills just before they got to Sage. She'd been careful to see that everybody nearby could hear what she said. It was enough.

Just to put a finishing flourish on it, Celeste said, "Oh my, Amos! Mr. Barby is right. It would be wicked of me to suspect a family you know so well. I'm sure they couldn't possibly be German spies."

A very satisfied Celeste looked over the one-year-old colts at the horse show. She had no trouble identifying the one she wanted. It was the finest looking colt she had seen since her days in Arabia. The colt's lineage was uncertain, but as Teddy Mack put it, "You can't judge a horse by its pedigree. The question is, will he trot?" She bid ruthlessly when he was up for sale. But somebody outbid her.

"Can't go any higher, Lovely," said Teddy Mack. "That's a mighty fine colt, but we'd have to sell the brownstone in New York. I'd like to meet the fella with that kind of money."

So would I, thought Celeste. She knew that like every one of her companions, Teddy Mack would get old and boring. But she never imagined him running out of money. Not when she wanted something so much as that colt. It put her in a real funk.

Later, Teddy Mack met up with some friends. It had something to do with a rancher's association. Celeste begged off and sat in her room pouting. She didn't lose often. When she did, she was in a fury for days. There was a knock at her door. Her maid answered, returning with a note.

Madame,

I hope that you are not too disappointed that I outbid you on the colt. In fact, we might be able to work out an arrangement. Might I presume to meet you in the lounge at eight o'clock this evening? Am I being indiscreet to suggest that you come alone? I'll find you. Another Judge of Fine Horse Flesh.

It was perfect. Teddy Mack wouldn't be back until eleven o'clock. There would be just enough time to charm her way into getting that colt after all. Pout ended, she began to plan her strategy.

It was twenty minutes before eight. She called for her maid "Bring me the belted tunic suit and the velvet evening hat that goes with it. Be quick. There isn't much time. I'll also have the black suede button shoes and carry the matching handbag."

Timing it so that she arrived slightly after eight, Celeste made a striking entrance into the lounge. The gentleman apparently hadn't arrived. The note hadn't said so, but she assumed it was from a gentleman, someone who admired her great beauty. Otherwise, why ask her to come alone? She found a small table with two comfortable chairs, seating herself in one. A tall gentleman entered the lounge. Like Teddy Mack, he wore a large Stetson hat that obstructed a clear view of his face as he strode toward her table. She demurely looked down as if it were of little consequence.

"Celeste, I presume?" he asked, looking down at her. "Or do you prefer Mrs. Barby these days?"

She looked up with a start. She knew that voice. "C'lestin! I might have known you'd show up at the wrong time. What are you doing here? I am expecting someone."

"Yes, 'Another Judge of Fine Horse Flesh.' That would be me."

"So it was you who bought him just so I can't have him. Now you've come to gloat," she sputtered. "What are you going to do with a one-year-old colt?"

"Give him to you," he said, smiling as he seated himself in the other chair.

Her eyes narrowed. "Give him to me? Why would you want to do that? You paid a fortune for that colt."

"He was mine to start with. If I choose to buy my own colt and give it away, what is that to you?" asked C'lestin.

"Give him to me? You never appear except tell me to repent and change my ways," she fumed. "You don't have to say anything. I can have the horse if I give you the Last Crystal. I can hear it coming," she let out an exaggerated sigh. Then in a mocking voice, she said, "You want the crystal to repair the earth. I should give it to you. If I do, I will grow old and die. Boo-hoo. But I will be filled with wonderful feelings about doing good. Tosh! Why should I want to repair the earth? The earth can repair itself."

Celeste sat back in her chair, glowering at C'lestin. "I am the most beautiful woman who has ever lived. I have enjoyed every minute of the life the crystals have made possible. Why would I want to throw that away so some forest will grow on an obscure mountain or some species of iguana will survive in the Galápagos Islands? Sorry, brother dearest, no deal. Keep your colt."

"You are very hard on yourself, Celeste," said C'lestin.

Celeste let out another great sigh. "Go on, get it over with. Give me the lecture and go away."

"There is no lecture, Celeste. The colt is yours. He needs a good home. I don't have the time to care for him and I know of no one who will give him more loving care than you will."

"What is the catch?" she asked suspiciously.

"No catch," he said. "I only outbid you to make sure you really wanted him."

"So why would you want to give me the colt? Why not give him to that Matthias boy you rescued from the fire? I know it was you who did it, just as I know you have put that crystal back in time where you think I can't get it. I'm not Immortal like you. If I don't have that crystal, I will die. You don't care about that, do you?" she taunted him. "All you want is to keep the earth going when you know as well as I do that the earth won't go on forever, crystal or no crystal. This sun we orbit is going to give out eventually no matter what you do. If you'd had your way, you'd have all the crystals and I would already be dead."

"I can't change the choices you've made, Celeste. I didn't come here to talk about that, I came here to give you a colt. Do you want him or not?" said C'lestin.

"Of course I want him, you idiot. But if you think I'll love you for giving him to me, think again. I'll take him because I want him and I won't owe you anything. Understood?" her voice was hard and unbending.

"Celeste, you can only give away love. You can't buy it back." With that C'lestin stood. "When you return to your ranch, the colt will be there. Be kind to yourself, sister. I love you, always have, always will."

Dumbfounded, Celeste watched him leave the lounge and walk out of the hotel. "Well, anyway, I get the colt."

"What was that again, ma'am?" asked a waiter. She hadn't realized she had spoken aloud.

Chapter 23

THE MOB

Amos Counts came home with a blue ribbon. When he told his father what the beautiful lady said, Mr. Counts snorted, "Hogwash!" That would have been the end of it except for Jimmy Logan from Cedar Hills who had a pig in the pen next to Amos and overheard Celeste.

Jimmy Logan's father, Jim, was a member of the American Protective League. He was one of the men who kept watch on German-American employees at the cotton gin. He was hopeful of catching a German spy, but so far, he hadn't had any luck.

"The lady is absolutely right," said Jim Logan. "There are German spies who've been planted in the United States for generations. I don't know what these Matthias people are tryin' to do, but they're out to serve the enemy. They probably feel pretty sure of themselves, hidden away in Sage. We'll put a stop to that."

A few days later the Matthias family sat down to supper. James was so famished he could hardly wait for Papa to say grace. It was baking day so they had a cold supper. Mama had been busy all day baking for the week. The smell of hot yeast buns, bread, fruit pie, and oatmeal cookies was tantalizing. Mama had set out cold chicken left from dinner. There was three-bean salad and a potato salad to go with it. Yeast buns were still warm, just waiting for him to slather them with butter and home-made berry jam. James took a drumstick and a mound of potato salad as they were passed around. He was about to help himself to three-bean salad when Papa said, "That sounds like a truck." Not many people drove trucks in Sage, just a few of the farmers were beginning to get trucks to replace their horses and wagons. Most of them lived around Cedar Hills.

Sure enough, a truck pulled into the yard and a man came hurrying up the porch steps. Papa went to the door.

"I am sellin' war bonds," the man said. "Our records show that you haven't bought war bonds."

"I don't believe I know you, Sir," said Papa politely.

"I'm Jim Logan. I represent the American Protective League. Not enough people are buyin' bonds to support the war effort."

"We are pacifists," replied Papa kindly. "We do not buy war bonds."

"Is that so?" sneered Mr. Logan. "Then I reckon we'll haveta buy 'em for you." Turning away from the porch he called, "Round up that prize bull, boys." He left Papa standing at the door.

Mama's face went white. James ran to the window to see a truck back up to their corral as another truck with men piled into the back pulled into the yard. Men began rounding up Big Red. Others jumped down off the bed of the second truck and began to help get him loaded into the truck. "No! Not Big Red!" James cried. "Papa, don't let them take Big Red."

"I'll ask them to take two of the other cattle instead, Son. If they're bent on taking some of our cattle to buy war bonds, there's not much we can do to stop them. But I'll try to reason with them," said Papa. A crowd was gathering around the truck. Still another truck pulled up. It was loaded with men, too. "This isn't about buying war bonds. James, get your Mama and Maggie out, like we agreed. Follow the escape plan. I don't like the look of that crowd."

Chapter 23

"Karl!" cried Mama. "Come with us. Let them do what they will. You can't stop them. Hurry."

"No. Get the children to safety. I'm going to ask them to leave Big Red." He was resolute. "James, do as I asked. Take Old Shep. Be quick about it."

With his heart in his throat, James hurried with Mama, carrying Maggie, to the basement cellar. They let themselves out through the cellar door that opened behind the house. Old Shep was right there waiting. It was if he knew what was needed. Old Shep led them through the garden and behind the tamarack trees that marched along their property on the side opposite the creek boundary. When they were well out of sight of the house, they cut back and took the road up to the Bates property, walking as quickly as they could.

They got to the Bates' house out of breath. Hank Bates answered the door. Taking his gun, he said, "Hannalore, I promise not to shoot anybody. But a well-placed shot in the air could get their attention. Come along, James. Nobody will know you aren't my son. You're safe enough with me. These men sound like hooligans from Cedar Hills. I'll go to the bank on it. Norma Jean, set off those flares like we talked about. Then take the car, get on up into Sage and let them know."

214

"We don't have time to saddle up, hop on behind me." Mr. Bates mounted his horse bareback, leaving the car for Mrs. Bates and Mama.

When they got back to the house one of the trucks was gone. Big Red was nowhere in sight. A crowd of men stood in a semicircle, facing Papa. He was stripped to the waist, hands tied behind his back.

A bunch of men came out of the house carrying pillows. "The rest of them must have high tailed it out of here," reported one of the men. "Can't find any evidence in the house, but we got the feathers."

"Well, they's destroyed the evidence or taken it with 'em. We shoulda surrounded the house first. Bring those pillows over here," yelled Mr. Logan. "Now Matthias, we are reasonable men. You tell us where you are hidin' the evidence of your work for the German government and we'll go easier on you."

"I'm a second-generation American citizen," said Papa calmly. His voice carried across the crowd. "I love this country and its constitution. I am proud to be a citizen of a country that has a Bill of Rights that guarantees religious freedom."

"Make him sing, 'The Star Spangled Banner,'" yelled somebody from the mob. There must have been thirty men in all. Some of them had guns. Mr. Logan was at the front of them all.

"That don't prove nothin'," yelled somebody else. "Let's jest tar and feather him and get it over with."

James watched in horror. A man with a bucket of pine tar stood looking at Papa. The men who had been in the house split open several feather pillows. They were actually going to paint Papa with pine tar and throw feathers on the tar. Papa stood there, taking the taunts, looking straight at Mr. Logan without answering back.

Ducking his head and pushing through the crowd before Mr. Bates could stop him, James ran straight up to Papa. He planted himself between Papa and men with the tar and feathers. "No!" he cried. "If you want to tar and feather somebody, take me."

"Son," said Papa calmly, but firmly. "Get out of their way. Stand behind me."

"Well looks like we've got the junior spy here. Make him dance for his Papa, Sam," said Mr. Logan. "Out of the way, boys." The men with the tar and feathers stepped back.

Sam was a tall man, carrying a Colt 45 pistol. He began shooting right at James' feet without hitting him, but coming so close James jumped to stay out of the way. The mob loved it, hooting and jeering at James as he danced to avoid the bullets. Eight shots and the man had to reload. James was sweating.

"Heck, this is better'n the pictures!" One of the men said, howling with laughter. He wasn't alone. The others cheered along with him. Sam started shooting again.

"Hold it!" came a booming voice from behind James. "This man ain't no traitor! I've got two sons in the army and I'll vouch for him. He's a good man and he's my neighbor. Y'all want to tar and feather him? You have to tar and feather me first. You ain't puttin' one hand on Karl Matthias."

Sam stopped shooting.

James was flabbergasted. Coming up from behind the barn was Mr. Higgins, the last person he'd have expected to stand up for Papa. Higgins took a stand next to Papa. Claude was right behind him, a sawed-off shotgun aimed at Sam. No wonder Sam had stopped shooting. Claude planted himself on the other side of Papa.

"You want to tar and feather him, you have to take me first," said Claude in a deadly calm voice. "You may shoot me, but I'll take two of you with me first, startin' with you, Mister." He pointed his gun straight at Mr. Logan now. "If you don't think I'm that good, try me."

The mob began taking a few steps back. James, who'd refused to step behind his father, still stood in front. He could feel the sweat running down his face.

"No Claude," said Papa, quietly. But his voice carried. "This is about non-violence. Shooting is against everything I stand for. Put the gun down, Claude. Please."

"If you say so, Mr. Matthias. But it would pleasure me to shoot the ground out from under that Big Shot's feet." Claude put the gun down.

Momentarily, the crowd was stunned. But soon it was back in action. "Heck, we got enough tar for all of 'em," laughed a man in front. "They're nothin' but a bunch of pantywaists."

Several things happened almost all at once. Two of the men in the mob stepped forward with brushes to help the man with the tar bucket. All three began dipping their brushes in the pine tar. James didn't say anything, he just stood there, looking at them without flinching, like Papa.

"Get out of my way, boy, or I'll tar you first," said one of the men.

James didn't say anything. He just looked at the man as he swiped a glob of tar across his chest. He could feel the warm pine tar seeping through his shirt. The other men began slapping tar on Mr. Higgins and Claude.

At the same time, Mr. Bates shot in the air twice. The startled crowd parted as he strode to the front, "Karl Matthias is my neighbor, too. The only reason I'm not shootin' the lot of you is out of my respect for him. If you want to tar and feather him, then you're gonna' have to tar and feather me first." Suddenly Mr. Taylor was there with his three sons coming from behind the barn. They all made a human wall in front of Papa.

"That's right," said Mr. Taylor, "And if you have enough tar and feathers, come and get us. We're standin' with Karl and his son."

"My folks have known Mr. Mathias for a long time and he doesn't agree with war and fightin' so you have no right to make him fight," yelled Frank.

"That's right!" yelled Jess.

The men with the pine tar were finished slapping tar on James, Claude, and Mr. Higgins. They slapped tar across Mr. Bates' shirt and moved on to the Taylors. Another couple of men followed with the feathers, throwing them in hands full so they stuck to the tar.

It was all happening with split second timing. Suddenly Mrs. Higgins was there, too. She planted herself right in front of the man holding the bucket of tar, bringing him to a momentary halt.

"Get that woman out of the way!" yelled Jim Logan. "Of all the cowardly things I've ever seen, hidin' behind women and chil'ren."

"Elsie, there's no call for you to be here," said Mr. Higgins, firmly. "Go home. This is men's business."

"I have every reason to be here," she said in a very loud voice, facing the crowd. "If you want to talk about cowards, every one of you men out there should look in the mirror. This man you are callin' a coward saved my husband's life. He risked his own life to pull him out of a fire! Karl Matthias didn't ask me to come here. If you ask him, he'd tell me to go home, just like my husband done. But I'm not goin' home 'til you go home, the lot of you. If you want to harm him, then harm a woman first. Then we'll see who the real cowards are!"

Suddenly there was a swirl of neighbors coming up from behind the barn. Paul Davis and his three boys joined the ranks flanking Papa on both sides. Mrs. Davis, who'd refused to stay at home, stood with Mrs. Higgins, linking arms with her. They positioned themselves in front of James and Papa. "If you put tar and feathers on this good man, you're going to have to tar us, too," said Mr. Davis. Right after him came Amos Counts and his father and older brother. Billy May and his father, Jake Hill and his father and two brothers, Danny Smith, his father and one of his brothers—the other two were in the army, Mr. Tipton and his wife and the preachers from both churches in Sage and their wives. The women linked arms with Mrs. Higgins and Mrs. Davis, making a line that stretched out in front. It seemed like everybody in Sage was coming. They completely surrounded Papa.

One of the men with a brush sneered. "We'll paint the lot of you," he said dipping the brush in pine tar again.

"You want to get yourself tar and feathered, then have it your way," said the other man with a brush. The mob began cheering. The men with the tar shoved the women aside and smeared pine tar on everyone they could reach. Men with the feathers followed, throwing them at the women and on everybody smeared with tar. None of the neighbors moved. Nobody said anything. Even the mob became quiet. All you could hear was the sound of tar being dipped and slapped on people.

Then Papa began singing, "My country tis of thee, Sweet land of liberty, Of thee I sing."

The neighbors beside and behind him joined, "Land where my fathers died, Land of the pilgrim's pride, From ev'ry mountain side, Let freedom ring!"

The man holding the tar bucket set it down. "You want him tarred do it yourself, Logan," he said. "I don't have the stomach for this anymore." Somebody else from the mob picked up the tar bucket and his brush. Just about everybody standing around Papa had a streak of tar across their front except for the women. Feathers were floating everywhere, some sticking to the tar, some sailing in the air.

Chapter 23

Then Norma Jean Bates drove up honking her horn with Mama and Maggie, Mrs. Taylor and their baby, Miss Hurley the teacher, Danny's aunt Inez, and a load of children stuffed into the car two deep on laps. Women and children were in the rumble seat and women and girls stood on the running boards. The mob opened for them in astonishment.

Some of the men in the mob began hooting and jeering as Mrs. Bates slammed on the breaks in front of the house and the women and children spilled out. A couple of men began throwing feathers at them and jeering. Everybody standing with Papa kept singing as the women and children joined them. They linked arms with the others standing around Papa.

Suddenly a man from Cedar Creek made his way up from the back of the mob and began singing with them as the second verse began, "My native country, thee, Land of the noble free, Thy name I love." Another couple of men from the mob stepped into the group and joined in the song, "I love thy rocks and rills, Thy woods and templed hills, My heart with rapture thrills, Like that above." Some of the mob turned and walked away. Two more Cedar Hills men joined the singing. Everybody around Papa kept singing. "Long may our land be bright, With freedom's holy light, Protect us by Thy might, Great God our King."

Mrs. Davis, who had a beautiful soprano voice, began singing, "O beautiful, for spacious skies, For amber waves of grain." As people joined in, "For purple mountain majesties," Mr. Logan walked away in disgust. Above the music, James could hear trucks pulling away. He realized that tears were running down his face. His was not the only face wet with tears.

James and Claude untied Papa as the last note of "America the Beautiful" died away. There was silence for a moment. Then a great cheer went up when everybody realized the trucks were gone.

Papa held his hand up for silence. "Nobody ever had better friends and neighbors," he said. "I can't thank you enough. Tonight you have shown that mob what a real American looks like, and what courage looks like. Dale and Elsie Higgins here have two sons in the army. John May, your oldest boy just enlisted. Two of the Smith boys are already serving in the army. Paul Davis' nephew and Earl's cousin is an officer in the army. Mr. Tipton's younger brother just reported for the draft and will do non-combatant service as a conscientious objector. We're all people who love this country because here in the United States we are free to be different. We're free to disagree with each other. And we're free to follow our conscience. This is the America I love. We're not perfect yet—we won't be until every American is free to be different." He paused, interrupting his own sermonizing. "And it looks like I'm one of the few who isn't covered with tar and feathers! How did that happen?"

Everybody laughed and clapped everyone else on the back, carefully avoiding the sticky tar and feathers that were globbed on most of the men and some of the boys. They told their different versions of what had just happened. People in Sage traded in Cedar Hills. They knew about some of the terrible things going on there. They followed the national news, too. They'd heard about what was being done to German-Americans in other communities. So some of the families privately agreed behind Papa and Mama's backs that if anybody ever got word of them being persecuted for being German-American and pacifist, they'd send up a flair. Everybody who saw the flair would send up another flair and head for the Matthias place ready to stand with Papa and Mama.

"These men didn't mean us women to come," said Norma Jean Bates. "But we couldn't stay behind. Besides, we figured we could go for the Sherriff in Cedar Hills if we needed to."

Paul Davis laughed. "I reckon over in Cedar Hills they'll think we've been celebrating the fourth of July again! You should have seen the flairs goin' up.

Hank Bates looked over the crowd. "We want to thank those of you from Cedar Hills who joined us. Looks like your comrades left you behind. I'll run you home with our thanks for stepping across the line and taking part, if somebody can give these women a lift home."

"Not till we've helped clean up," said one of the Cedar Hills men. There were five men from Cedar Hills. They shook hands with Papa and apologized.

By this time Mamma and Norma Jean Bates had been in the house and returned with a bucket of lard. Most of the men and boys had jackknives and were already helping each other carefully scrape tar and feathers from their clothing. Papa scraped James' shirt for him and helped everybody he could. The women passed around lard for them to rub into their clothing as soon as most of the tar and feathers were scraped away. James rubbed lard over all the places where the tar had hit him. It would soften the rest of the tar and keep it from hardening on his clothes until he could put them in a tub to soak.

The men and children who weren't scraping tar and feathers swept up feathers using broom weed or whatever they could get their hands on to brush them into piles where they were gathered and put in a gunny sack for burning.

Mama and the women went back in the house and busied themselves making lemonade and moving their kitchen table to the front yard. Mamma had them set out everything she had baked, including the bread and what was to have been supper. James saw his plate with the untouched drumstick and realized he was hungry. They made a regular party of it. Folks from around Sage who'd seen the flares kept coming up and joining in until it seemed like the town must be empty. More food appeared and was added to the table, the story was told and retold.

Finally, and much later, as people started home, James extended his hand to Claude. "Thanks for what you did, Claude," he said. "That was really brave."

Claude took his hand and shook it firmly, looking him in the eye. "He'd have done the same for us if we needed him and I reckon you would, too."

As everybody left, Papa put his arm around James. "Son, that was a brave thing you did. I was hoping to protect you and Mama and Maggie by drawing away their attention while you escaped. Looks like you all ended up protecting me."

Mama said, "What Elsie Higgins did may have been the bravest of all because she went against Dale. But I think he was proud of her in the end. There was something about seeing all those men, women and children standing up to the mob that really got to some of those men from Cedar Hills, even the ones who didn't join in with us."

"There is always hope that people like those men in the mob can be repaired," said Papa.

"Some people have been bent so badly that they won't change. But we can keep hoping."

"And praying," said Mama, "and trying to love them."

"What about Big Red, Papa?" asked James, fearfully. He pulled off his shirt to put in the wash tub Mama had already filled with hot water. In all the excitement he had forgotten about Big Red.

"I couldn't stop them, Son," said Papa sadly.

Mama put her arms around him. Tears ran down her cheeks. "I'm so sorry, James. I'm so sorry."

Chapter 24

THE OKLAHOMA NATIONAL STOCKYARDS

Teddy Mack pulled his big new yellow roadster into the parking area at the Oklahoma National Stockyards. It was a spontaneous decision. He'd been in the city for a meeting of the National Stockmen's Association. Celeste was keen to make the trip because she wanted to see if she could hire a trainer for her new colt. She doted on the colt. She wasn't willing to trust him with just anybody, but a famous trainer had just retired to Oklahoma City.

Once they were in the City, she had little trouble charming the trainer into agreeing to visit their ranch in Texas. He promised to work with the colt before making a decision to come out of retirement. So she was in an elated mood and didn't fuss when Teddy Mack said he wanted to look in on the auction on their way out of the city the next morning.

"Lovely, if you want to stay in and get a little extra beauty sleep, I'm goin' early," said Teddy Mack. "I want to get there while they're still unloadin' some of the trucks. That's the best time to pick up information on what's for sale. I'll come back for you."

Celeste didn't want to wait. She didn't even complain when they left their hotel at daybreak.

It was a bit dusty as they made their way around the pens holding cattle that would be up for auction. Celeste had on her yellow travel duster and a big matching hat with a veil. Even with the veil, she attracted a good deal of attention as they wove in and out among the trucks that were pulling in with cattle for sale. She almost caused a traffic jam so many drivers were gawking at her.

Some of the cattle would be sold to farmers and ranchers. Others were destined for the packing plant. Teddy Mack wasn't interested in buying. He just liked a good auction. And he loved the gossip that went on around buying and selling, though he wouldn't have called it gossip.

A truck that was in line waiting to get to one of the holding pens caught Teddy Mack's eye. "That looks like Big Red!" he exclaimed. "What do you think, Lovely? Reckon he'd be about that size by now."

Dust was flying everywhere. Celeste held the veil from her hat securely in place with a gloved hand. "So it does," she said. "That Matthias boy is a little sneak. I thought as much. He promised to tell you if he planned to sell Big Red."

"Well, you could be right, but I don't think so. He didn't strike me as that kind of boy. I'm goin' to have a word with that man drivin' the truck. Maybe it isn't Big Red."

When Teddy Mack asked, the man snickered, leaning his head slightly out of the truck window. "No I ain't the owner. You might say I'm representin' the owner. This here bull is bein' sold for war bonds, if you get my meanin'."

"No, I don't get your meanin'," said Teddy Mack politely. "'Spect you'll have to illuminate me."

"German fellow over in Sage refused to buy bonds, so we figured we'd do it for him," said the driver. "We're sellin' his prize bull for him. All the money goes to buyin' bonds."

"You don't say," said Teddy Mack. "I'd call that stealin'."

The driver sneered. "We call it supportin' the war effort. You one of those yellow-bellied Krauts or what?"

"I will disregard that comment," said Teddy Mack. "Besides, I am not wearing my pistols. How much you reckon you'll get for him?"

The driver named a figure. "Tell you what," said Teddy Mack, getting out his wallet. "I'll give you that in cash and save you the trouble of payin' the auctioneer and holdin' fees."

The man scowled.

"And I'll save you the trouble of dealin' with the law," Teddy Mack added. "There's a US Marshall in attendance who happens to be a personal friend of mine. If you get my meanin'. The way I figure, he'd be right interested in how you acquired this animal. I reckon you don't have any papers on him, either."

"You're bluffin', big shot," said the man, lifting his hat off his head and running his fingers through his hair.

"Suit yourself," said Teddy Mack. He started to return the money to his wallet.

The man hesitated for a moment as if he were doing some calculations in his head. "Take him," he said at last. He took the money Teddy Mack offered and stuffed it in his wallet.

"Oh, brilliant!" said Celeste, smiling with satisfaction. "You wanted Big Red all along."

"I'm not keepin' him, Lovely. I'm givin' him back to that boy."

"You're what?" Celeste couldn't believe her ears. "And how do you plan to get him there?"

Teddy Mack turned to the driver. "How's about you drive me over to where my truck is parked? I'll sweeten the pot for you." He pulled out another couple of dollars.

Celeste looked at Teddy Mack as if she thought he were out of his mind. "Truck?" He winked at her.

The man's truck was still idling, "Well hop in," he said. "I ain't got all day."

But before he knew what had happened, the driver was sitting on the ground, hands tied behind his back with Teddy Mack's great big, expensive silk handkerchief. "I'm borrowin' your truck and takin' Big Red back where he belongs," said Teddy Mack. "I don't call it stealin', I call it liberatin' stolen property. You can consider my silence on the subject of your rustlin' this bull as payment for use of your truck. I'll leave it at the bus station in Cedar Hills for you. Here's five dollars. You can use it to buy more war bonds or you can use it to get home or both. Suit yourself." He threw five dollars at the man and began turning the truck around. "See you back at the ranch, Lovely. You have a key to the car and you know the way. You can untie the man if it suits you or you can leave him here for somebody else to find." With that he stepped on the accelerator and peeled out, nearly taking the side off of one of the holding pens as he made a U-Turn.

It suited Celeste to untie the man. She pumped him for information before she let him go, promising to drop him at the bus station in the city. She was a bit put out with Teddy Mack for returning Big Red, but she was very satisfied to learn that when the driver left the Matthias property with Big Red, Karl Matthias was about to be tarred and feathered. She took wicked pleasure in imagining how upsetting that would have been to James. Her plan for revenge had worked.

As for the man, he'd never had five dollars of his own all at once. Celeste had him thoroughly mesmerized by the time he got to the bus station. It cost him about fifty cents for bus fare to Cedar Hills. And he had plenty of money for sale of Big Red to give to The American Protection League for war bonds. He didn't see fit to spend the rest of the five dollars on bonds. He figured it wouldn't be necessary to furnish too many details about what had actually happened, either. So he deducted what he figured he'd have had to pay for a holding pen and the auctioneer, too, keeping it for himself.

Chapter 25

SOUTH ON MERIDIAN POSTAL HIGHWAY

Celeste stopped back at the hotel long enough to freshen up. It had been terribly dusty at the stockyards. She asked for a packed lunch to take with her, too. Shortly after, she drove out of the city feeling satisfied. Things were going her way. Never mind if Teddy Mack insisted on returning that animal to the Matthias brat. Her plan may have failed, but the crystal was still in her power even if it wasn't in her hands. The open road was ahead. She intended to enjoy herself to the fullest.

Leaving Oklahoma City, she took the Meridian Postal Highway south. She would take a slight detour to Sulphur where she would spend the night in the splendid Artesian Hotel. She might take a day or so to enjoy the park and the mineral waters Sulphur was famous for, before driving on down into Texas.

It was almost time to stop and enjoy her hamper lunch when she heard someone humming. It sounded like the wildly popular "At The Dark-town Strutter's Ball." The humming came from the back seat, then a male voice sang out, "Goin' to dance out both my shoes, When they play the Jelly Roll Blues." She took a quick look. Nobody was there. But the singing continued, accompanied by unseen snapping fingers. She pulled the car over to the side of the road and turned to have a look at the back seat. Nobody was hunkered down there. But the singing and finger snapping continued. There was only one possible solution to this puzzle. "All right. Make yourself visible, Sandastros. It has to be you," Celeste ordered. Her mind raced ahead. Sandastros. She hadn't heard from him more than a couple of times since she'd taken the sixth crystal from its hiding place. She hadn't expected to hear from him again until the time came for the Last Crystal to be opened. Sandastros, immortal, greatest of sorcerers, her teacher. *I wonder what he wants*, she thought.

The singing stopped. Her picnic hamper, sitting on the back seat, seemed to open on its own. A sandwich floated in mid-air. A bite disappeared from it.

"I mean it. Stop that right now," demanded Celeste. "That is my lunch you are eating."

The tip of a brightly colored porcupine hair crest appeared first, followed by a shaved scalp on either side of the crest. A head and face were followed by broad shoulders. A cape was draped over one shoulder. Finally, a man wearing the dress regalia of the Chickasaw Nation, complete with formal deerskin moccasins appeared, munching on her sandwich.

Celeste was nonplussed. "What are you doing here dressed in that ridiculous costume and singing 'Darktown Strutter's Ball?'"

"You expected a chant? How narrow minded." The man calmly finished chewing a third bite of Celeste's sandwich.

"This is totally ludicrous," Celeste sputtered.

"This was the Chickasaw Reservation, after all. I thought it best to go native."

"This hasn't been the Chickasaw Reservation in decades," said Celeste. "It's a state park."

"Stolen from the Chickasaws," said the man, licking butter from his fingers.

"It was all perfectly legal, I'm sure," said Celeste.

"It always is," said Sandastros, smirking.

"When did you suddenly become a goody-goody?" Celeste demanded.

"*Au contraire* my dear, I'm very proud of the part I played in that deception. I deceived the Chickasaws and the US government. Well done on my part."

"Why am I even arguing about this?" stormed Celeste. "All you are doing is making a spectacle of yourself." The occasional car or horse and wagon passed. People gawked at them.

A pick-up truck pulled up alongside the car. Two men sat in the front. "This Injun givin' you trouble, Ma'am?" asked one of the men, looking goggle-eyed at Celeste.

Sandastros answered before she had a chance, "Good afternoon Gentlemen. My chauffer is reluctant to drive through Indian territory." He spoke in a very posh British accent. "I assured her that it is perfectly safe. We natives are thoroughly civilized. Thanks awfully for stopping, though. Good of you."

It was no good disputing him. He'd find some way to weasel around anything she said. There was a time when she could have bested his magic, but that was long ago. Celeste gave the men a radiant smile, and waved, hoping to get rid of them. As they drove away, she said, "The Chickasaws are an ancient people. They were civilized before you ever paid them any attention. Must you ridicule everyone?"

"But my dear, it is what I do," he grinned.

"Really, Sandastros, this is too much," she said. "And eating my lunch, to boot."

"I am astonished. The Queen of Spectacles is complaining about attracting attention?" Sandastros chortled. "Oh, but it is me getting the attention, not you. That explains it."

"All I want is a quiet drive. You're making this into a circus."

"No. No, not a circus," he said. Then, giving her a radiant smile, he added, "But if that's what you want, we'll need elephants. One positively cannot have a circus without elephants, can one?" He'd finished off the sandwich. Now he took a bite out of her apple.

"You're impossible!" said Celeste, pulling back on to the road. She looked into the rear-view mirror. Two elephants were following behind. She stepped on the accelerator, but the car crept along at a walking pace. "Sandastros! Stop this craziness," she shrieked.

"We're almost in town. We mustn't disappoint these wonderful people," said Sandastros. A signpost said, "Welcome to Pauls Valley." People seemed to appear from everywhere, walking along with the big yellow roadster, waving. A chimpanzee with a toy steering wheel now sat in the passenger seat, waving at the growing crowd and steering the car this way and that. Gripping the steering wheel, Celeste

238

tried to get the car on course. Nothing happened. The crowd fell back to keep out of the way. She slammed on the breaks. Nothing happened. The chimp with the toy steering wheel was in complete control of the car.

"There, pull into that vacant lot," directed Sandastros. The chimp steered the car into the lot. Stepping on an imaginary brake, he brought them to a stop.

"I'll bet you've forgotten how to do your high wire act," said Sandastros. "You used to be spectacular when you were younger. I daresay you're getting a bit old for that sort of thing now."

Already rattled, Celeste took the bait. "I'm as good as I ever was."

"Seeing is believing," said Sandastros. "I dare you."

No longer vacant, the lot was filled with men busily putting up a circus tent. Standing in line behind the car were three elephants, two camels, a dozen clowns, six white horses, and an ostrich along with a gathering crowd of men, women, and children. A band entered the lot from the other side. Behind the band were three pretty girls carrying a large banner that read, "Free Circus, Today Only. See the Magnificent, Daring Celeste on the Trapeze."

"Well, don't you have a dressing room for me?" she demanded.

"You'll do it then? Of course you will. Marvelous. I'll be your catcher," said Sandastros. Now he was dressed as a Master of Ceremonies with a top hat and full head of jet-black hair. Getting out of the back of the car, he saluted the crowd. A red caravan wagon with yellow wheels pulled into the lot. It had Celeste painted on the side. Pointing to it he asked her in his irritatingly sweet voice, "Are you sure you dare to do this darling? If you fall and hurt yourself, there isn't anything I can do for you. You are, after all, a mere mortal." He laughed a beautiful, musical laugh.

"Shut up," said Celeste angrily, getting out of the car.

"You'll find your old costume in the caravan," said Sandastros, waving to the crowd. "I hope you can still fit into it."

She did not grant him the dignity of a reply. Celeste had no trouble fitting into her costume. She'd performed with a circus in Europe several decades ago and after a quick trial on a three-foot high wire the clowns played with, she found that her balance and timing were as good as ever. She wasn't worried about injury. She had water from the sixth crystal with her and the Last Crystal in her power. Sandastros would give nearly anything to get his hands on it. He wouldn't let her fall. He knew full well that if she died, the Last Crystal would implode.

The tent was packed with people. The show was spectacular beyond belief. The astoundingly beautiful and daring Celeste's performance on the high wire left the crowd breathless. The dashingly handsome man who served as ringmaster thrilled the crowd when he threw aside his cape and began scaling the rope to the trapeze. After a few dramatic swings to warm up, he hung by his knees and caught Celeste as she came flying through the air to meet him. Several times he deliberately let go of one hand and acted as though he would drop her. The crowd loved it, but she was furious. She was performing without a net. He just wanted to make her look bad and steal the show. He couldn't. The crowd adored her. She upstaged him every time.

There was free popcorn and cotton candy, too. Unfortunately nobody could remember anything about the circus after it was over, except for one little boy and his younger sister who weren't allowed in. The little boy, whose name was Jimmy, saw the parade just as Sandastros was getting out of the yellow roadster.

"Excuse me, Sir," he said, mustering up all of his courage. "When will the circus begin?"

"Soon, young man," said Sandastros kindly. "Why do you ask?"

"I want to go home and get my little sister. It wouldn't be right for me to see the circus and her to miss it."

"Oh no," said Sandastros with the greatest sympathy. "What a fine brother you are. Do go get your little sister. We'll save a place for you."

Just before the circus was to begin, Jimmy and his sister came running as fast as their legs would carry them. "Sorry, the tent is filled to capacity," said a man who stood at the entrance. "No one else is permitted in, by order of the ringmaster."

"What is this?" asked Sandastros, appearing at the entrance.

"Sir," said Jimmy, bravely, "You said you would save a place for us."

"I think you misheard me. I said I would save a place for you." Sandastros smiled at Jimmy sympathetically. "I said nothing about your little sister. There is a seat for you right next to where I sit when I'm not performing. I saved it especially for you. Come on in. Your little sister will have to go home."

Jimmy didn't hesitate. "Then Sissy can have the seat and I'll wait out here for her. It wouldn't be fair to make her go home after I got her hopes up."

"That won't do at all," said Sandastros, looking firm. "The seat is for you. Take it or leave it. The circus is about to start. If you wanted your sister to see the circus you should have come on time. Now off with you both." He didn't even offer them any popcorn or cotton candy.

They stood there in disbelief. They watched as the elephants went in a side entrance. A beautiful lady walked from a red caravan, disappearing into the tent after the elephants.

"I don't think that man is very nice," cried Sissy, tears streaming down her face.

"No, he isn't very nice," said Jimmy. "And he didn't tell the truth either. He promised."

Jimmy and Sissy got off better than anybody who saw the circus, though. Besides the fact that that nobody could remember it, every one of them got sick from eating enchanted popcorn and cotton candy. People talked about an unusual stomach ailment going around, but nobody could figure out what caused it. A farmer just outside of town complained that three of his cows, a couple of pigs and his team of white plow horses were missing. The sheriff found them along with a neighbor's prize turkey and little goat wandering on the other side of town in a confused state. The goat was reported to have developed an usual interest in cars after that, jumping into the driver's seat whenever he had a chance.

Jimmy got a good scolding for telling whoppers when he and Sissy got home. Their father had just been past the vacant lot on his way home from work. "The only thing I saw was a lady in a brand new fancy yellow car talking to some man dressed like a dandy."

Later that night, when their mother came to tuck them into bed, Jimmy said, "There really was a circus, Mamma. And that man said he would save a place for Sissy and me."

"And he wouldn't let us in," said Sissy, tears welling up in her eyes.

"I am so sorry," said their mother, giving them each a kiss on the forehead.

"Why doesn't Daddy believe us?" asked Jimmy.

"I guess some things are just unbelievable," said their mother, kindly. "It is hard to imagine anybody being so mean. In fact, I'll bet that a man that bad has a really bad circus."

"Yeah," said Jimmy, "Maybe it was a really bad circus."

"And you know what?" asked his mother. "Your Daddy and I are going to take you and Sissy to the Oklahoma State Fair efore it closes this fall. We've been planning it. They have all kinds of things to do and you can see animals, too. We'll buy cotton candy and popcorn. How about that?"

"How about that!" exclaimed Sissy, eyes shining.

"Yeah," said Jimmy. "That's better than a bad old circus."

*****

The fact is that by the time Jimmy's daddy passed the vacant lot, the last dazed member of the audience had left the tent and wandered home, trying to remember where he'd been. Everything had vanished: tent, elephants, clowns, camels, chimpanzee, and all. Sandastros and Celeste were left standing next to the big, shiny new yellow roadster.

"I guess I showed you a thing or two," said Celeste. "The audience loved me. You have to admit I was spectacular."

"They loved me even more," Sandastros gave her an annoying smile. "I was sensational. But that's just me: amazing and sensational."

"I am driving on into Sulphur. You may take yourself and your circus wherever you like. I've had enough of you," said Celeste.

"Before you go, I thought that perhaps you would like to explain how you managed to let our crystal be taken right out from under your beautiful nose for the second time?"

"At last, the real purpose of your visit," said Celeste, bristling, "First of all, it isn't our crystal, it is my crystal. Secondly, nobody can open the boxes that hold it without me knowing. C'lestin cannot open them and neither can you."

"You are so wrong, my beautiful, mortal," said Sandastros. He smiled, showing his perfectly even, gleaming white teeth. "I taught you everything you know about the dark arts. You

245

couldn't have taken those crystals without me in the first place. So yes, they are our crystals. You remain under the illusion that they belonged to you. But it's just that, an illusion."

"You are so predictably unpredictable," Celeste sneered. "I don't see you for hundreds of years and you show up with a circus, whining. You deceived me, Sandastros. You took advantage of my ignorance of the ways of the world. You made me believe that I had to give up my magical powers and immortality in order to live among mortals. You never cared a fig for me. All you wanted was the crystals and to put a stop to my sorcery. You knew that I far surpassed you in magical powers. Yes, you were my teacher, but I went far beyond what even you can do. You were afraid that I would displace you."

"You are so right, my dear. I did deceive you very badly, didn't I?" Sandastros laughed a silky-smooth laugh. "It was one of my better pieces of work. Poor Celeste. The immortal who wanted to be pretty like mortal women. Now she is so very, very pretty and so very, very mortal. Without the water from those crystals she would be 'poof,' gone. Her only purpose in life is to be young and beautiful."

"And your only purpose is to spoil and deceive," Celeste retorted.

"I had far better plans for those crystals. You have wasted all of them on yourself, all but this last one. I think you should give it to me."

"You are getting tedious," said Celeste, getting in the car. "I've given you everything we agreed to. One drop from each crystal, that's all. You agreed to the terms because you thought you could best me at the magic. The Great Deceiver was deceived."

"Thank you for the compliment," said Sandastros. "I am great, but I am only a student of the Great Deceiver. The student is not greater than the master, something you refused to learn."

"Stop trying to bully me. You should know by now that it doesn't work. I am leaving." With that, Celeste started the big yellow roadster.

"Don't forget, darling," said Sandastros before she could drive away. "I will unlock the secret to that spell you used to bind the Last Crystal. Now that I know all it takes is a child, I shall find a child. I may not do it today. I may not do it tomorrow, but no matter. Time is of no consequence—oops! Time is of no consequence except to you." He laughed again, softly, musically, infuriatingly.

Containing her rage, Celeste replied, "But first, you have to find it. Perhaps you should ask C'lestin. I'm sure he'd be delighted to help you." With that she drove away. Behind her, the vacant lot was suddenly completely empty. Sandastros had disappeared.

Chapter 26

A TRUCK RETURNS

Teddy Mack hadn't had so much fun since he was a kid. The first thing he did when he was out of sight of the man who owned the truck, was pull over and take Big Red on a walk around to give him a stretch. Big Red didn't resist. He was well trained. "Anyways, you and me go way back. I figure you must know me," said Teddy Mack, giving him a rub behind the ears. Big Red took a long drink from a stock tank outside the holding pens. "Remember when we first met? You'd just been in the Best of Show. Shoot, you were the best in the Best of Show as far as I was concerned."

Teddy Mack kept up a steady stream of conversation as if he were talking to his best friend. Nobody paid any attention. But as they made their way back to the truck, several people offered to buy Big Red on the spot. Teddy Mack grinned proudly at each offer and said, "I just picked this fellow up myself. You can't blame me for wantin' to keep him."

After Big Red had a good walk and another drink of water, Teddy Mack led him back into the truck. "You're goin' home, Buddy." He patted Big Red on the back of the head. It took awhile to get to Sage. Teddy Mack gave Big Red a couple of breaks on the way. Big Red could have made the trip without a break, but Teddy Mack was in the mood to baby him. By the time he got to Sage, it was straight up noon and dinnertime. He pulled into the Matthias driveway singing to himself.

James was the first to hear the truck. His heart almost skipped a beat. He was afraid it was another bunch of men from Cedar Hills. Then he saw Big Red standing in the back of the truck. "Papa, Mama, come quick. It's Big Red! It's Big Red!" he called rushing out the door.

Teddy Mack got out, a big smile stretched all over his face. "Look who I ran into at the stockyards this mornin'. Thought you might like him back, James. Reckon he was ready to come home."

James couldn't get the back of the truck open fast enough. He climbed over the side and jumped in with Big Red, throwing his arms around him, burying his face in his neck.

Papa and Mama and Maggie came running right after James. Mama said "Mr. Barby, you must stay for dinner. I'll put on an extra plate while James lets Big Red out. No arguments, now. I won't take 'no' for an answer."

Teddy Mack grinned. "Reckon I wasn't consciously tryin' to show up at dinner time. But you gotta admit it was mighty good timin' on my part."

James walked Big Red back to his place in the pasture. Big Red seemed to be as happy to be home as James was to have him. He frisked around the pasture like a bucket calf, running back up to James and butting him gently in the stomach. James threw his arms around him and gave him a good ruffing behind the ears. Then Big Red was off again.

James would have stayed there all afternoon. But when Papa called, he realized that he was ravenously hungry.

Teddy Mack told them the whole story of how he'd found Big Red. They laughed until they were nearly in tears. He said it was the best meal he'd had in years as he finished off his pie. Papa took him around to see the herd and invited him to stay on for supper and spend the night if he wanted. But Teddy Mack said he needed to return the truck and catch the train to Ft. Worth that evening. "You've got to go all the way around the world to get to Ft. Worth by train," he said. "So I'd best get started. I like train travel, though. One of these days I want to travel all the way across the US of A by train. If this durned war is ever over, that is." He shook his head sadly as he pushed back from the table. "I'm real sorry about what happened to you folk. I couldn't disagree with you more about war, but every man and woman should have a right to follow their conscience."

Mama sent him off with a boxed supper to eat on the train. "If this here box has some of that fried chicken and a piece of that blackberry pie, my life may be in danger," teased Teddy Mack. "The Dalton Brothers would of shot a person for less than that. Be the next great train robbery. Folk will be gunnin' for me just to get at my supper."

Still laughing, they watched him pull out of the drive. Arm around James, Papa said, "Sometimes things turn out all right, don't they, Son?"

James grinned. "Yeah, sometimes they do." He liked Mr. Barby. But he was relieved that Celeste hadn't come along.

For her part, Celeste spent a restless night in Sulphur, Oklahoma. She hated admitting it, but Sandastros always unnerved her. She admired him long ago when he was her teacher. But the time came when she saw that he was like a beautifully wrapped box with nothing in it. He was a great sorcerer, but she had become greater because he didn't focus. He spent too much time being just plain mean to others and thinking of dirty tricks to play on unsuspecting people. She, on the other hand, was a woman with a purpose. Any damage done to others was done because they insisted on putting themselves in the way. It never occurred to her that she too had become a beautifully wrapped box with very little left inside.

She decided not to stay over, leaving early the next morning. The thought of Sandastros lurking nearby took all the fun out of lingering at the mineral springs. Once she turned west toward Fort Worth, she was tempted to keep driving all the way to California. But she remembered the colt and headed for the ranch. Sandastros could follow her with a herd of elephants for all she cared. He was powerless to do anything about the crystal. And she had a colt to get ready for the Triple Crown. *I wonder if he missed me?* she thought as she turned on to the road to the ranch. She wasn't thinking of Teddy Mack. She was thinking of the colt.

Chapter 27

UNEXPECTED ENDINGS

"You must have grown a foot since last time I saw you," said Teddy Mack, shaking hands with James. "Give me those bags."

"Thanks, Mr. Barby," said James, handing him one of his suitcases.

"You're goinna be finishin' high school here pretty soon, aren't you?" Teddy Mack asked.

"In a couple of years, Sir. I'll be in grade eleven in the fall."

"Time flies so gal durn fast a fellow can't keep up with it," said Teddy Mack. "How was the train ride?" He led James through the train station in Albuquerque, New Mexico.

"The train ride was really swell!" said James.

"Once you get past the Rockies there isn't much to look at besides scrub bush, prairie dogs, and coyotes." Teddy Mack chuckled. "Well, maybe the occasional jack rabbit."

"I used to live in Albuquerque," said James, suddenly remembering as he looked around. We took the train from Albuquerque to Kansas City. I must have been about six-years-old then. I'm not real sure. We were moving to Kansas City. It was right after Old Shep came. We had to put Old Shep in a crate to go with the bags. I didn't understand why he couldn't just ride in the coach with us."

Teddy Mack laughed. "Knowin' Old Shep, I'd say it's likely that he had better manners than some folk that take the train. How is he, anyway? He's gettin' up there in years now."

"He's as frisky as ever," said James, smiling to himself. It was something his parents marveled at, too. But there were some things best left unsaid.

Leading James out to where his brand new, shiny black pick-up truck was parked, Teddy Mack said, "Mark my word, train travel is the wave of the future. It's a great way to go. Reckon I'll sink a little money in railroads, be a good investment. Celeste always liked the train. She liked havin' a private car, though." He heaved James' suitcases into the back of the truck. "For my part, I like mixin' with the *hoi polloi*. Nobody is more inter-restin' than ordinary folk. Hop in while I give this thing a crank and we'll get her goin'. I didn't get a truck with one of those fancy electric starters like they have on the cars. Figure the exercise is good for me."

James jumped in as the engine started.

"Listen to that! This baby purrs like a kitten once you get her goin'." Teddy Mack grinned as he got behind the steering wheel. "So how's everybody at home? With the war over, I hope things have settled down a bit for your folk." He didn't give James a chance to get a word in. Without so much as pausing for breath, He stepped on the clutch, shifted into reverse and backed up with alarming speed.

"Sure is nice for you to come out. I've been rattlin' around by myself ever since Celeste left. I told your folk she's in Paris for the summer, but turns out, she's in Paris for good." He sighed. "After her prize colt had to be put down it was like somethin' snapped."

"She had a colt?"

Teddy Mack slammed on the brake, stepped on the clutch, and shifted out of reverse. "That's why we were in the stockyards that time Big Red nearly got auctioned off. We'd been to find a trainer for her colt. They have this horse show every year at the State Fair. Best anywhere. She had her eye on a colt that was up for auction. Somebody outbid her, but she ended up gettin' it anyway. Celeste has a way of gettin' what she wants. I can't figure out for the life of me how she pulled that deal. But that's Celeste." Stepping on the accelerator, he took off like a shot out of a gun, tires screeching. "Learned how to drive yet?"

"No sir, we don't have a car—yet," he added, though James wasn't convinced they'd get one any time soon. Papa seemed content with the horse and buggy even though just about everybody else in Sage was driving now.

"'Spect I'll have to teach you, then," said Teddy Mack. He whipped around terrified pedestrians and oncoming cars as they left the station. "As I was sayin' about Celeste, she doted on that colt. Thought she had one that could win the Triple Crown for sure. Hired herself a fancy trainer. He knew his stuff, too." Teddy Mack slammed on the brakes, throwing James to the dashboard, as a man led a donkey out into the street. He kept right on talking. "They did really well in the early races, but never got as far as the Kentucky Derby. Poor fella broke his leg. Celeste just couldn't get over it. She wanted to go back to Europe, so I gave her the Paris apartment, her freedom, a pile of money, and my blessing. Course she's a lot younger than me. I'm getting' old and fossilized and she looks just as pretty as the day I met her." He let out a big sigh. "Sometimes you just have to let go."

"I'm sorry to hear about the colt," said James, keeping one hand on the seat of the truck and the other on the dashboard. He couldn't help wondering how Celeste could be so upset over losing a colt and not think twice about having his birth parents killed. He couldn't think of anything good to say about her, so he kept his mouth shut.

Teddy Mack didn't seem to notice. He turned out of town, leaving a spray of gravel as he sped onto the road. James held on, afraid they'd turn over. Stepping down on the accelerator and the clutch, Teddy Mack shifted gears. "I'm gunnin' this baby. She'll go durn near 40 miles an hour. Let's see what she can do on the open road." James held on to his seat as they flew down the road. Teddy Mack didn't seem to worry about which side of the road he was on. James prayed they wouldn't meet anybody coming in the opposite direction.

"I guess she always had a bug in her." Teddy Mack swerved as a truck appeared, barely missing a jackrabbit that apparently imagined he'd be safe if he froze. At the last minute the jackrabbit went bounding off. James wondered if the rabbit was as terrified as he was.

"I never did know anything about her upbringin'. But she sure was fixated on lookin' pretty. Never knew anybody quite like her. Bein' married to her was like tryin' to keep a rainbow in a jar. There are some things that can't be done, no matter how hard you try. Anyways, that was then. This is now. I decided to invest in some of this new land out here in the middle of nowhere and build up another ranch. And I figured that if I'm gonna make that train trip clear across the US of A, this is the time to do it while I can still put one foot in front of the other."

James was excited about the train trip, too. Just about the time for school to end, Mama and Papa got a letter from Mr. Barby. He asked if they could spare James sometime before summer was over. He wanted to take him on a train trip across the United States. They would travel to California by the southern train route, then all the way back from Los Angeles to Chicago on the California Limited before heading for the East Coast.

James would never have agreed except the letter said that Mrs. Barby was in Paris for the summer. So he jumped at the chance. Mama and Papa wanted to pay his expenses, but Mr. Barby wrote that he couldn't make the trip alone. Having James with him was cheaper than hiring a companion. So it was settled. It was the beginning of August when James took the train from Dodge City to Albuquerque.

It was a wonderful trip. James loved every minute of it. One of the best parts was remembering. From the time he set foot in the train station at Dodge City, he began to remember things. He remembered making a trip from Albuquerque to St. Louis. Mamma bought sandwiches from the cart on the train. He could see Mamma and Daddy's faces as they looked at little Gracie asleep in Mamma's arms and back at him. It was like all the pieces of the gigantic puzzle of his life before he was James Matthias were falling into place, small details that Mr. Nichols and Miss More and her brother hadn't been able to tell him.

They went to California, then all the way back to Chicago and on to Washington, D.C., ending in Baltimore before they started back. They got off the train in Dodge City on their return from Baltimore. Teddy Mack had arranged to have his pick-up truck waiting for them at the train station. From there they drove down to Sage, stopping to visit Alabaster Caverns. "Geologist friend is studyin' 'em. The Caverns will be a real tourist attraction one day."

There are some things you can't talk about. James couldn't talk about his mother going into the crystal room with Mr. Nichols and opening the black alabaster box that held the Last Crystal. But it was on his mind the whole time he was there. He stood in the crystal room imagining what it must have been like for her. There was no longer a black alabaster carin, but he could imagine it. "Grace," he said.

"What's that Son?" asked Teddy Mack.

"My mother's name was Grace. She got to visit here once."

"That's a pretty name," said Teddy Mack. "Did you ever see anything like that streak of black ala-

baster? I have in mind getting' myself a black alabaster chess set. You know how to play chess?"

"No sir," said James.

"Reckon I'll have to teach you. Improves
logical thinkin'. Ought to require it in school, then
maybe we wouldn't have so durn many fools trying
to run the government." Teddy Mack talked on.

James, caught up in remembering, barely
heard him. Mr. Nichols once said, "It isn't by
chance that your mother was named Grace." He
wasn't sure he understood, but he had a feeling
he'd grow into it.

"What did you say your family name was,
before you were adopted?" asked Teddy Mack.

"Henry," James said. "My father was David
Henry and my mother was Grace Willis Henry.
My father was a geologist and cartographer and
my mother was a teacher and an artist."

"Well heck, why didn't you say so before?"
asked Teddy Mack. "I got somethin' you ought to
have. Reckon I'll send it to you when I get back to
Albuquerque." He wouldn't say what it was.

On the way south, Teddy Mack decided it
was time for James to learn to drive. It made
the trip take a little longer and they had some
bumpy moments while he learned how to step
on the clutch and shift gears without throwing
the two of them onto the dashboard or through
the windshield. Teddy Mack was actually better

at teaching than he was at driving. When they arrived in Sage, James was the one driving. He was good enough to drive with one hand and wave with the other.

"Mr. Barby, you ought not to have done that!" chided Mama when James brought the pick-up to a halt in the front yard. "Now he will be lobbying for us to get a car. The thought of driving terrifies me." But she didn't fuss when Mr. Barby let Maggie sit on his lap and drive around the yard.

James couldn't wait to tell Mama and Papa about the trip and, most of all about himself. That part—telling about himself—had to wait. Mr. Barby stayed on for a week, doing chores with Papa and complimenting Mama on her cooking. He kept them entertained with stories about life on the ranch in Texas and his plans for the ranch in New Mexico. "I reckon we can make this an annual event, James," he said as he threw his suitcases into the pick-up the morning he left. "Shoot, there's more places you can get to by train every day. Once you're out of college you might make a pretty good railroad man yourself."

James didn't miss the pained look Mama gave Papa. He knew they wanted him to go to college, but times were hard after the war. He'd heard their worried conversations about how they were going to be able to pay for new farm equipment and where the money would come from for James to go to college. He wanted to be an engineer, but Oklahoma State University at Stillwater was a long way from home and it would cost more than they could afford for him to live away from home. Besides, Papa needed him on the farm. If he left, they'd have to have a hired hand. He wasn't sure what the future held.

It was late August, almost time for school to start, when Miss More and her brother Otis drove up. Like James' family, they still drove a horse and buggy. Before he left for the train trip, Miss More made James promise to tell her all about his trip with Teddy Mack when he returned. He'd gone to see her, but she was away. Mama said she'd been away most of the summer.

Mama asked them in for pie. James talked a bit about his trip. But as they were finishing Mama's delicious chocolate meringue pie, Miss More said, "James, I want to hear more about your trip, but Otis and I came to tell you something. We are just back from Sacramento, California."

"We had our own train trip," said Mr. More, adding in a more serious tone, "I was reluctant to take Leoti and the children because we didn't know what we were getting in to. Not everybody is accepting of Cherokee people and I didn't want to put her and the children through that."

"Our brother sent me a telegram right after you left with Mr. Barby," said Miss More. "You may remember that our twin brother and sister turned out badly."

More than badly, thought James.

"We lost track of them completely," she continued. "I didn't know they had any idea where I live. Neither of us had heard from them for years. The telegram was out of the blue. Our sister Ruby was very ill and was asking for us. Our brother wired money for Otis and me to make the trip. Of course we went."

"Junior met our train," said Mr. More. "We wouldn't have known him. He was clean and well spoken. He's even learned to read. It turns out that Junior and Ruby started a security company. He trains the officers and she ran the business end. H & R Swathe Company, it's supposed to be the best on the West Coast. He even has one of the railroad accounts."

"They started a new life out there, James," said Miss More. "Junior—Hiram, he goes by Hiram now—married a real nice woman. They have five children—including twins, a boy and a girl. They named the twins for Otis and me." There were tears in her eyes. "They are as nice as any children you could ever meet."

"Ruby lived with them," said Mr. More. "She had her own successful business besides running the business with Junior. She taught women how to defend themselves. But Junior's wife, Ellen, said that she was always tormented by her past."

James could feel anger welling up. *She should be tormented by her past. She is respon-*

sible for my parents being dead. He clenched and unclenched his fists out of sight under the table, feeling as if he might explode.

"When we got there, she was very near death," Miss More continued.

"James," said Mr. More gently. "I heard her confession. She wondered if she should try to return to Oklahoma and give herself up for her crimes. But she was too weak. Some people would probably say that both she and Junior should have been brought back to Oklahoma to be hanged. It would satisfy the law. But I'm not so sure it would satisfy justice." He sighed. "I don't know. Myrtle and I can't see any good purpose in it. Ruby paid for her crimes in the anguish she felt for the rest of her life. And Junior has turned himself around. What good would there be in leaving a widow and five children in order to satisfy the law?"

James could see Mama and Papa nodding in agreement. But he wanted to see Ruby and Junior hanged. They should have to pay for the terrible thing that they did to his parents and would have done to him and Gracie if it had gone their way.

"James," said Miss More quietly. "This must come as hard news for you. Ruby didn't know that you and Gracie survived the fire until we told her. It was a great comfort to her. She wanted to make amends. The fact is, she has been making amends since they left Oklahoma. Ruby helped start an orphan and foundlings home in Sacramento. She left part of her estate to them. She left some to Otis and me for our work. But once she knew you are alive, she wanted the rest to go to you, for your college education, if you'll have it."

James was so stunned that he suddenly didn't know how to feel, much less what to say. He wanted to scream, to run outdoors and scream as loud as he could until he couldn't scream any more.

"James, she wasn't pretending it would make things right," said Miss More looking at him intently. "You see, when she killed your mother, something happened to her. Your mother asked her to at least spare you and Gracie. She didn't expect that you would ever be able to forgive her, but she hoped you will allow her to do this for you."

Mr. More added, "We were there with her for nearly a month. She died peacefully. Ellen said she was more at peace than she'd ever been since she had known her."

Tears were streaming down Miss More's face. She tried to catch them with her handkerchief, but it was wet. Mama gave her another, reaching for one to wipe her own eyes.

"It's up to you, James," said Mr. More gently. "You don't have to take the money. Don't try to decide now. It is too fresh and it brings up too many raw feelings. You have time. But I will say this, our life on this earth is too short to spend it bearing a grudge and too long to live without forgiveness."

****

Chapter 27

At that moment, Celeste sat in her apartment in Paris looking in the mirror. She frowned. The slightest hint of wrinkles had appeared in the corner of her eyes. Ringing for her maid, she looked more closely.

"You called, Mademoiselle?"

"I need my black leather case," said Celeste.

The maid took it from the wardrobe where Celeste kept it. "Thank you. You may go," she said, taking it from the maid. She unlocked the case. Inside was a black velvet box. It, too, was locked. Carefully, she removed a cut-crystal vial. She hadn't used it in years. Taking the stopper from the vial, she dabbed the tiniest drop on her temples, behind her ears, and wrists as one might apply perfume. But this was no perfume. It was life-giving water from the sixth crystal. *There is enough here for at least a hundred years,* she thought. *If it weren't for that interfering brother of mine there would be no occasion for concern.* The Matthias boy had mentioned a map. *I wonder*, she thought. Perhaps it was time to have a look at that map.

She returned the vial to the velvet box, locking it and setting it inside the leather case. As she locked the leather case, her eye fell on a card propped against her dressing table mirror. She'd stuck it there when it came, forgetting it. She read it again. "Dearest Celeste, I am saddened to know about the colt. I know you loved him. I'm so very sorry. Love no end, C'lestin."

"Why did I keep this simpering piece of sentimental sop?" Ripping it into pieces, she flung the bits toward the wastebasket where they fell like snow. "This isn't over, C'lestin! I will have it back!" she shrieked.

"Temper, temper, darling!" said the reflection in her mirror. "It makes your face go all wrinkly." Looking out at her was a devilishly handsome face.

"You can stay out of this, Sandastros."

"And miss all the fun? I think not. I shall take the liberty of looking in on you from time to time now that you've put our crystal at risk." The face vanished as quickly as it had come.

*****

One late afternoon not long afterward, James stood looking at his red abalone shell. He thought about Kipo'mo's promise to take care of Gracie, and about Gracie, growing up in a world so different from his own. He thought about the summers they had spent together since his first visit after he almost gave Celeste the Last Crystal. They were about the same age now. He looked forward to telling her about Mamma and Daddy and more about their life together when they were James and Gracie Henry when Mr. Nichols came for him next. He never knew when it would be, almost always when there was a free afternoon. And he always got home in time for chores.

When you've spent forever putting together a complicated puzzle without being allowed to look at the picture on the box, it is a satisfying feeling to put the final pieces in place. *I must be the luckiest boy in the whole world*, he thought. *I have had two families who love me.* He hurried downstairs to help with the chores before supper.

Mama and Maggie had supper ready when he and Pa brought in the milk. "I fried the chicken for supper, Ames," Maggie announced, setting a platter on the table. She was growing up, but she still called him Ames. It would always be her special name for him.

James picked her up and lifted her off the floor. "You're almost too big for me to do that now, Maggie!" he puffed, putting her down.

"Pretty soon I'll be big enough to lift you up in the air," she said as she scooted her chair up to the table.

"There was a package for you in the mail, today, James," said Mama. "It's from Mr. Barby."

After dinner was over, the table cleared, and the dishes washed, James opened the package. Inside was a large book, *Discovering the American West* by David Henry and Grace Willis Henry. There was an inscription inside, "To Teddy Mack and Lucille Barby with many thanks for your hospitality and deep appreciation for your continuing support." It was signed, D. Henry and G. W. Henry. There was a photograph of the whole family tucked between the pages, too. Mamma is holding him on her lap and Daddy is holding baby

Gracie. They are all smiling. James could hardly believe it. "He knew them! Imagine that. And this a picture of them—of us!" He held the picture almost reverently before passing it around.

"Read the letter, Ames, read the letter," said Maggie.

It was short.

Dear James,

Grace and David Henry were good people. I have a packet of letters from them somewhere in my stuff. Grace used to write every Christmas. Always wondered what happened to them. They owned a house in St. Louis—Grace grew up there. You ought to have your Papa look into it. I'll dig around and see if I can't find the letters and send them to you.

Your friend, T.M.B.

"Oh James, what a wonderful gift," said Mama. She looked at Papa, smiling. There were tears in her eyes. "Now you really do know who you are."

"I am James Henry Matthias and I am proud of it," James said, giving Mama a hug.

A few days later, James Henry Matthias took a walk into Sage with Old Shep. He couldn't shake the feeling that Old Shep had been trying to tell him something. When they got into town James sat down on the steps of the church where he was found, arm around Old Shep. "This is where James Matthias got started," he said to

269

Old Shep. The years since had come and gone so quickly. They sat quietly for awhile. James looked around at the familiar town he had come to love. He knew everyone in it and just about every nook and cranny.

"You know, Old Shep, I think I will accept that money for college. I haven't forgiven Ruby Swathmore or her brother. I don't think I can do that, at least not yet. But I can have the grace to allow Ruby to do something good."

Old Shep looked at him in his knowing way. He approved.

"Mr. Nichols said that it wasn't by chance that my birth mother was named Grace. I wonder if that's what he meant?"

Wagging his tail, Old Shep put his head in James' lap. "You're trying to tell me something, aren't you?"

Old Shep looked up at him, snuggling closer.

"You're going away, aren't you, back to Mr. Nichols. He needs you to help somebody else."

It was if he understood Old Shep perfectly without any words being necessary. "I don't need you so much now. But oh my, I'll miss you! Mama and Papa will miss you. And what about Maggie? She'll need you when I go off to college."

Old Shep looked at him with kind eyes.

"I know, she has me whether I'm here or away." James sighed, struggling to figure out what he actually felt. He was sad, but he also felt at peace. Old Shep had been with him longer than he ever imagined possible. "I suppose that if you must go, you must. But this isn't forever, is it? I will get to see you again sometimes? At least when I go see Gracie?"

He buried his face in Old Shep's soft coat for a moment. Then they started back home. They were just past the canyon bridge when James realized that Old Shep was no longer with him. "Good-bye-old friend," he said. "And tell Mr. Nichols that you can come get me if you need me!"

You never know, he thought, smiling to himself.

MAPS

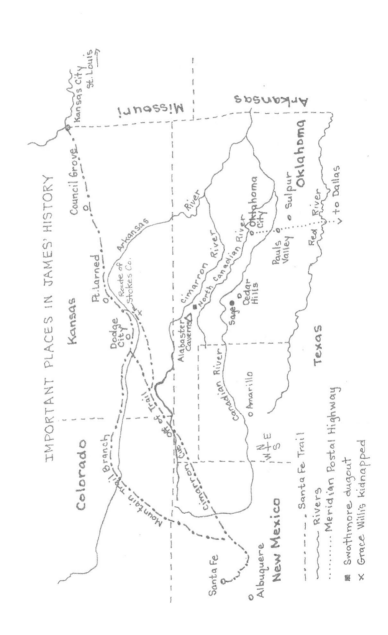

IMPORTANT PLACES IN JAMES' HISTORY

Colorado
Kansas
Missouri
Arkansas
Oklahoma
New Mexico
Texas

Kansas City
St. Louis
Council Grove
Pt. Larned
Arkansas River
Route of Stokes Co.
Dodge City
Cimarron River
North Canadian River
River
Oklahoma City
Sulpur
to Dallas
Pauls Valley
Red River
Cedar Hills
Sage
Alabaster Caverns
Canadian River
Amarillo
Cimarron Cut-off
Mountain Branch
Santa Fe Trail
Santa Fe
Albuquere

N
W E
S

----- Santa Fe Trail
—— Rivers
.... Meridian Postal Highway
▣ Swathmore dugout
✕ Grace Willis kidnapped

274

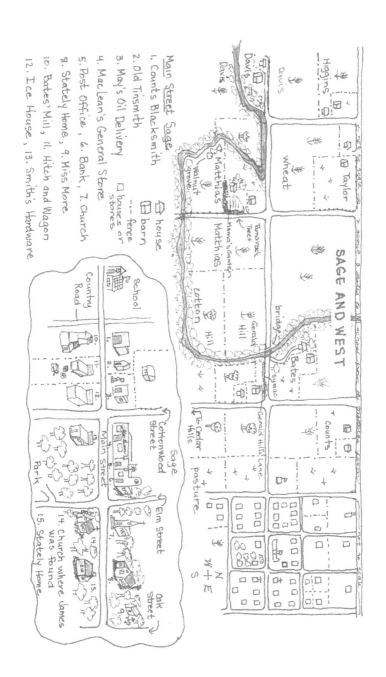

Main Street Sage
1. Counts Blacksmith
2. Old Tinsmith
3. May's Oil Delivery
4. MacLean's General Store
5. Post Office, 6. Bank, 7. Church
8. Stately Home, 9. Miss More
10. Bates' Mill, 11. Hitch and Wagon
12. Ice House, 13. Smith's Hardware

□ house
□ barn
--- fence
□ houses or stores

SAGE AND WEST

14. Church where James was found
15. Stately Home

N
W + E
S

ABOUT THE AUTHOR

Frances Schoonmaker draws on family stories and childhood memories of being reared on a farm in Western Oklahoma to write the second book in *The Last Crystal Trilogy*.

She attended public schools in Oklahoma until her senior year in high school when the family moved to Aberdeen, Washington, where she graduated from high school. Dr. Schoonmaker graduated from the University of Washington in Seattle and taught elementary school in suburban Seattle; Portland, Oregon; Nashville, Tennessee; and Baltimore County, Maryland before completing graduate studies and becoming a professor at Teachers College, Columbia University in New York. Now "Miss Fran," as the neighborhood children know her, lives in Baltimore, Maryland with her family.

ABOUT THE BOOK

The second installment of *The Last Crystal Trilogy* is even more engaging than the first as Grace's son, James, sets out on a journey full of danger, discovery, memory, and maturity. Schoonmaker skillfully and meticulously weaves even more history into this story, as we watch World War I unfold and witness how individual liberties can be so easily and tragically curtailed in the name of narrow-minded nationalism masquerading as patriotism. An important message for today perhaps.

Once again, the fantasy and magic driving this tale are the glue that keeps it enchanting and mysterious, but this volume adds more historical depth to the brew. Thankfully, Schoonmaker has also captured the danger of the Old West in wonderfully tense scenes without dragging the reader through violent, gore-ridden shoot-outs. There is also a delightful humor to this story in moments that are well-placed to move the plot and balance the emotion. I so look forward to seeing how this

story continues in the final volume.
—Kimberly Younce Schooley, Secondary School Teacher, Bishop Mackenzie International School, Lilongwe, Malawi

The Red Abalone Shell is one of those books that will keep you up late reading to find out what happens next. It is easy to get caught up in this engaging story that follows James after he is found on church steps with his beloved and loyal dog Old Shep. While James loves his adoptive parents, a pacifist German-American couple, he is eager to know more about where he comes from beyond his fragments of memories. The adventure that follows is filled with memorable characters and vivid settings. Woven throughout the story are fascinating historical details about life in the United States on the brink of entering World War I, which will intrigue anyone interested knowing more about this time period. I look forward to sharing *The Red Abalone Shell* with my students. I know that they will also be quickly caught up in James' adventure and not be able to put it down.
—Jennifer Goodwin, Assistant Principal, The Salk School of Science, M.S. 255, New York City Public Schools

The Red Abalone Shell is the perfect story for any middle grade reader who loves fantasy, mystery, historical fiction, and adventure all in one book. This second book in *The Last Crystal Trilogy* is the perfect companion to the first book, *The Black Alabaster Box*, or as a stand-alone novel. The book is set during early 20th century American life. Historical accuracy is obviously paramount to Schoonmaker and lessons on inclusivity and bullying are seamlessly woven in to create a story with rich detail and life lessons. Children won't even realize how much history they are learning while reading this epic tale.
—Angela J. Horjus, Head Librarian of the Lower School Libraries, Glenelg Country School, Ellicott City, MD

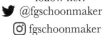